FLIP DOLLS
& OTHER TOYS
That Zip, Stack, Hide, Grab & Go

⚡ LAURA WILSON ⚡

FLIP DOLLS & OTHER TOYS

That Zip, Stack, Hide, Grab & Go

LAURA WILSON

LARK

An Imprint of Sterling Publishing
387 Park Avenue South
New York, NY 10016

ISBN 978-1-4547-0248-1

Library of Congress Cataloging-in-Publication Data

Wilson, Laura.
  Flip dolls & other toys that zip, stack, hide, grab & go / Laura Wilson.
-- First edition.
    pages cm
  Includes index.
  ISBN 978-1-4547-0248-1
  1. Dollmaking. 2. Textile crafts. I. Title.
  TT175.W553 2013
  745.592--dc23

                                                        2012040186

Distributed in Canada by Sterling Publishing
c/o Canadian Manda Group, 165 Dufferin Street
Toronto, Ontario, Canada M6K 3H6
Distributed in the United Kingdom by GMC Distribution Services
Castle Place, 166 High Street, Lewes, East Sussex, England BN7 1XU
Distributed in Australia by Capricorn Link (Australia) Pty. Ltd.
P.O. Box 704, Windsor, NSW 2756, Australia

For information about custom editions, special sales, and premium and corporate purchases,
please contact Sterling Special Sales at 800-805-5489 or specialsales@sterlingpublishing.com.

Email academic@larkbooks.com for information about desk and examination copies.
The complete policy can be found at larkcrafts.com.

Every effort has been made to ensure that all the information in this book is accurate. However, due to
differing conditions, tools, and individual skills, the publisher cannot be responsible for any injuries, losses,
and other damages that may result from the use of the information in this book.

Manufactured in China

2 4 6 8 10 9 7 5 3 1

larkcrafts.com

TABLE « of » CONTENTS

Introduction

I adore the humor contained in a computer covered in buttons. I love bringing idioms to life—like being swallowed up or coming out of your shell! I find the similarity between a button joint and a wheel axle irresistible. And I revel in the dual nature of a zipper mouth, in which the teeth of a zipper become crocodile teeth.

It's fun to approach sewing with this playful spirit, but you can also learn a lot when you play with what you make. When you fidget with a stuffed object, you learn to see it from all sides. And oftentimes you experience the thrill of having your expectations turned inside out.

I grew up watching my mother and grandmothers sew, and I learned to knit and cross-stitch at a young age. However, I didn't begin to think about sewing seriously until I saw a toy that belonged to my niece. It was a monkey that turned into a hippo. I loved the clever way the monkey hid snugly inside the hippo—then with a quick flip, the monkey was out and the hippo tucked away. I flipped it back and forth repeatedly. The movement of it fascinated me, and I was hooked.

Years later, when I was at home with my own daughter, I began sewing in earnest. I decided to make a flip doll. My first one was a cat and chicken. The chicken's head was kind of square, and I really struggled with the construction. But it was a start! I made other toys for years but kept coming back to the flip dolls. Eventually, I hit on a way to make the doll flip inside out instead of upside down. This change made the doll easier to assemble and easier to flip, while still keeping the form versatile enough for characters with fun details. After working out a few more kinks, I finally had a way to make the doll I'd been thinking about for almost a decade!

That's the kind of thought and tinkering that went into these designs—all of the patterns in this book are the result of playful inspiration. And each pattern contains the potential for surprises, from choosing a wild fabric or surprising color combination to creating your own variation of the design. In fact, I've included suggestions for ways you can playfully approach projects throughout the book, and tips for designing your own flip doll, zipper-mouth toy, and turnover doll.

I had fun making these toys, and I hope you do, too!

GETTING STARTED

tools & materials

Let's get started! First you'll need a space to work in and some basic supplies. All of the tools and materials listed here won't be needed for every project, but the ones in the Basic Sewing Tool Kit are essential for most. These are the tools that you'll use over and over again, so go ahead and get the good ones! On the following pages, I'll go through everything in more detail.

• •

basic sewing tool kit

Sewing machine
Iron
Sharp fabric scissors
Small scissors
Paper scissors
Straight pins
Sewing machine needles
Hand-sewing needles
Embroidery needles
Tape measure or ruler
Water-soluble quilting pen or chalk pencil
Turning and stuffing tools

• •

TOOLS

SEWING MACHINE

While almost any of these projects can be sewn by hand, toys need to be able to stand up to lots of wear and tear, and a sewing machine will ensure that your seams are strong. You can get by with the most basic machine, but you might also want one that has a zigzag stitch and a buttonhole function for some projects.

IRON

You'll need to iron your fabrics before cutting them, and for many projects you may need to keep a hot iron available to press seams as you sew. This will help make the assembly neat, and you'll be less likely to make mistakes. You may think this is a step you can skip, but do yourself a favor and don't.

SHARP FABRIC SCISSORS

If you do much sewing, you'll want to get a pair of sharp scissors specifically for cutting fabric. But to keep them sharp, don't use them for anything else! Cutting fabric with dull scissors makes messy edges and can be quite a chore. You may also want a pair of small scissors for cutting threads and making notches in seam allowances.

PAPER SCISSORS

Your basic craft scissors will do just fine for cutting out templates. If you have them around, you'll be less likely to use your fabric scissors.

PINKING SHEARS

These fabric scissors are for cutting a zigzag edge in your seam allowance. They aren't completely necessary for most projects, but they will keep the raw edges of your fabrics from unraveling, which helps the fabric, and the toys, last longer.

PINS

Straight pins are great for pinning your paper templates to fabric or pinning two pieces of fabric together. If you're the kind of person who likes to just wing it, that's okay. But have some pins around anyway, because chances are you will need them eventually.

Perching Birds (page 85)

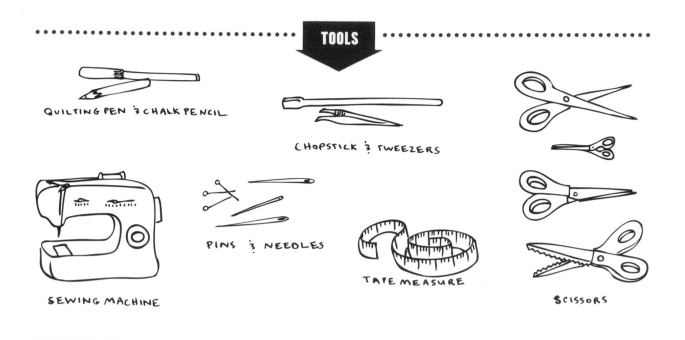

QUILTING PEN & CHALK PENCIL

CHOPSTICK & TWEEZERS

SEWING MACHINE

PINS & NEEDLES

TAPE MEASURE

SCISSORS

NEEDLES

All of the projects in this book can be sewn with a universal sewing machine needle. You should change your needle after every project, or at least every other project. Make sure your needle matches the weight of your fabric. You'll also need hand-sewing needles and embroidery needles (the same as a hand-sewing needle but with a larger eye) for most projects.

SEWING TAPE MEASURE OR RULER

Sometimes you'll need to measure small lengths of fabric. For these projects, they will usually be small amounts, so either a tape measure or a ruler will do.

QUILTING PEN OR CHALK PENCIL

Occasionally you will need to mark on your fabric where you plan to cut or embroider something. A water-soluble quilting pen allows you to draw on the fabric, and then simply rinse away the marks later. Be sure to follow the instructions given by the manufacturer so you don't accidentally set the ink. You can also use a chalk pencil and dust away the chalk later.

STUFFING AND TURNING TOOLS

You may want to buy stuffing tools such as hemostats or a stuffing fork. These work well for stuffing into small corners or down long skinny tubes. However, most of the time you can do just fine with household items like a chopstick and a pair of tweezers. These tools can also be helpful for turning projects right side out, especially those long skinny legs. For weighted fillers (see page 14) you may want to use a funnel and a spoon.

MATERIALS
FABRICS

When choosing fabrics, you'll want to consider color, texture, and weight. Some guidelines are below, followed by a brief description of different types of fabrics you may want to use.

Color

Most projects look great with two different but coordinating fabrics. Consider pairing a solid with a print, or a neutral with a bright color. Remember that busy prints, bold colors, and high contrasts are more exciting, while simpler prints and solids, softer colors, and monochromatic color schemes are more calming. Consider which one is a better fit for your project.

Texture

Similarly, try including one smooth fabric and one soft or rough fabric in a project, like quilting cotton with fleece or corduroy. If your project has a lot of trims, keep your fabric choices simple. Try to create a little variety without being overwhelming.

Weight

Unlike color and texture, it's important to use fabrics of a similar weight within a project so that the fabrics will stretch evenly and the seams will lie neatly.

Types of Fabric

✎ Quilting cottons will work well for all of the projects in this book, although sometimes another fabric may be recommended. These are a great choice because they come in a wide variety of colors and prints, and because they have little stretch or nap, they're easy to work with.

✎ Synthetic fleece, flannel, wool, or faux furs can add softness and furry texture to animals. Be aware that some of these fabrics stretch more in one direction than another. In this case, you will need to position your templates with the direction of the stretch in mind so that it doesn't distort the shape. (For example, position the fabric so that a long skinny section, like a tail or leg, will stretch to be

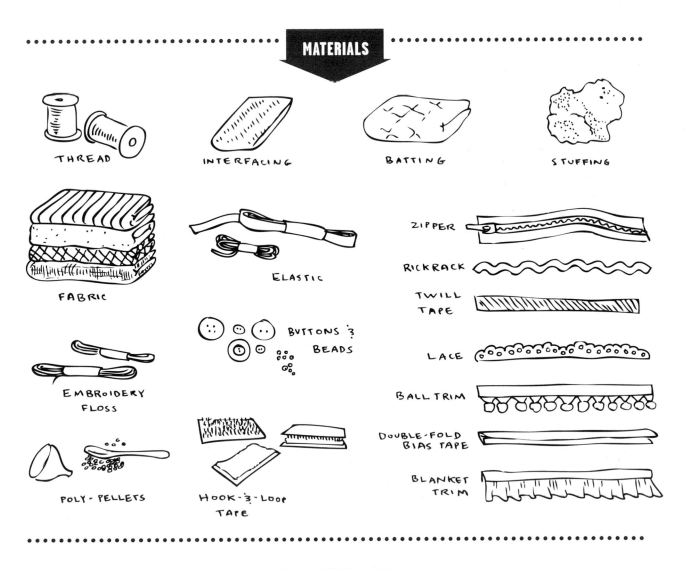

MATERIALS

THREAD

INTERFACING

BATTING

STUFFING

FABRIC

ELASTIC

ZIPPER

RICKRACK

TWILL TAPE

EMBROIDERY FLOSS

BUTTONS &
BEADS

LACE

BALL TRIM

POLY - PELLETS

HOOK-&-LOOP TAPE

DOUBLE-FOLD BIAS TAPE

BLANKET TRIM

wider rather than longer. This will look natural when it becomes three-dimensional.) A little stretch is also more forgiving around curved seams.

🖉 Corduroy, twill, and denim are sturdier fabrics that also add different kinds of texture. These work well for toys that need to be more durable than others. You may need to switch to a heavier-weight sewing machine needle for some of these fabrics.

🖉 Linen, cotton sateen, and apparel-weight fabrics will fancy up a project with their rich textures. However, these are often lighter weight. They wrinkle more and require more careful handling, so use them sparingly. You can strengthen and stabilize these by first applying a fusible interfacing to the wrong side.

FILLERS

There are several types of fillers, and each one may be made of a variety of materials. Here's a quick guide to your options.

Stuffing

Stuffed toys use a lot of stuffing! The most common option is synthetic polyester fiberfill, which is inexpensive and washable, making it well suited for children's toys—or any toy you might get dirty. Some natural options include wool, cotton, or kapok. These feel wonderfully soft; however, they either can't be washed (wool) or should be washed on a gentle cycle and line-dried (cotton and kapok) to prevent them from compacting. They are better suited for projects that don't get dirty or squished (which doesn't apply to very many toys).

Batting

This is the soft layer that goes inside blankets and comes in rolled-up sheets. A few projects in this book will call for batting instead of stuffing to pad flat items. Use low-loft batting for all of these projects, because high loft will be too thick. It's commonly available in polyester and cotton. Both can be washed and dried, but the polyester adds a bit of stiffness to your project while cotton batting makes a softer project. I prefer the stiffness of polyester fiberfill for the Bright Ideas Computer (page 73) and the wings of the Winged Horse (page 60), and the softness of cotton for the Peeka-

boo Turtle (page 48) and flip dolls. However, either will work for any of these projects.

Weighted Fillers

Weighted fillers not only add heft to a toy, but they create a different kind of movement as well. Plastic beads or pellets are durable and washable, and they have a nice weight. They are inexpensive and easily available at most craft stores. Natural materials like beans and rice can attract bugs and get moldy if exposed to moisture. Buckwheat hulls are a good natural option that won't attract bugs; however, they can't be washed, and so shouldn't be used in toys that will get dirty.

TRIMS AND OTHER NOTIONS

Trims are the spice of sewing! They can add pizzazz to any boring project. Some of my ideas have come from thinking about how I can use a fancy trim or a hot pink zipper. I like to keep lots of these on hand at all times, so I collect them at discount bins and yard sales. If you don't already have some in your stash, go ahead and get some!

Felt

Craft felt is inexpensive and comes in lots of colors. Wool felt is lovely to touch. Either way, because they don't fray, both types of felt are great for making appliqués that can quickly dress up any project.

Clear Vinyl

You can buy clear vinyl at craft stores, but because you'll only need a small amount, try cutting a piece from something you already have. Sheets and blankets often come in zippered vinyl packaging, which is perfect for the Nuts 'n Bolts Robot (page 64).

Rickrack, Lace, Ribbon, Twill Tape, Ball Trim, and Similar Trims

These decorative trims can either be sewn into a seam or topstitched onto a surface for different looks. They come in every color and size, and you'll find millions of uses for them. They are often used to define clothing by creating belts, collars, and hems. They can also be used in surprising, unconventional ways, such as for antennae, dragon spines, and caterpillar feet.

Bias Tape and Blanket Trim

These long strips of fabric are cut on the bias and specially folded to finish raw edges. These can be sewn by machine or hand and create a finished and decorative look when an edge can't easily be hemmed.

Buttons and Beads

Buttons and beads come in a wide range of colors and sizes. White and black buttons make good eyes, and colorful seed beads can easily be sewn on for quick decorations, as in the Good Times Watch (page 70).

Zippers

They may seem scary at first, but zippers are easily sewn in with the use of a zipper foot. The zipper foot attachment is inexpensive and available at

age appropriateness

When making toys for children, especially those under three, keep in mind these safety tips:

» Avoid using buttons or other small trims that could be pulled off and swallowed. Try embroidering the eyes instead of using buttons.

» If you stuff a doll with plastic beads or other objects, double-stitch the seams.

» Never give a child a toy with long strings that could cause strangulation.

» Use washable fillings for children's toys, such as polyester fiberfill.

» Be wary of any trims that might contain lead, including items that are metal or painted. If you aren't sure, look for an alternative.

Bouncy Bunny (page 54)

most sewing stores—just make sure you get the right one for your sewing machine. Slip it on in place of your regular presser foot, and you can quickly sew a zipper mouth that's sure to delight.

Embroidery Floss
Embroidery floss, readily available at craft and fabric stores, is a six-stranded thread that comes in a wide range of colors. Embroidery is a quick way to add child-safe eyes and other facial features to toys. You can also use it instead of appliqué to add fun details to any project.

Interfacing
Interfacing is sewn or fused to the wrong side of fabric to add stiffness and stability. Fusible interfacing is easy and inexpensive. Simply follow the instructions on the package. The Bright Ideas Computer (page 73) and Cheshire Cat (page 36) call for fusible interfacing.

Elastic
Elastic comes in several forms, including cord and tape that can be sewn into a project to make it stretchy. All of the projects with elastic in this book use cord elastic that is sewn into the seam easy peasy!

Hook-and-Loop Tape
Hook-and-loop tape is an easy way to make a closure. It comes in rolls with two strips of tape: one with hard hooks, and the other with soft fuzzy loops. You can topstitch the tape onto your fabric right over the hooks and loops. You may want to double-stitch the seams to make it secure, because the tape will be pulled apart over and over.

Fabric Glue
Glue made especially for fabric is durable but will feel flexible instead of crunchy like other glues. It's handy for securing any joints, appliqués, or accessories that will receive a lot of wear.

Cheshire Cat (page 36)

techniques

What follows are some guidelines for the techniques used to make the toys in this book. If you already know most of the Basic Techniques below, use the first section as a quick refresher to fill in any gaps. However, some projects call for unique skills that are defined under Special Skills. Each toy will list any special techniques it requires in case you need to refer back to them.

BASIC TECHNIQUES

ENLARGING TEMPLATES

The templates are included in the back of the book beginning on page 124. Before you begin, you will need to enlarge them. The easiest way to enlarge a template is on an office or library photocopier. If the enlarged template is bigger than a sheet of paper, you may have to print it onto two sheets and tape them together. Then cut out each piece. Store them in a plastic bag or file folder for future use.

CUTTING OUT PATTERN PIECES

Once your templates are ready, pin them to the appropriate fabrics. Be sure to use enough pins to keep the fabric or paper from shifting. Then cut out along the edge of the paper. If you have a complicated piece and find it difficult to cut along the paper, you can first trace the outline with a water-soluble quilting pen or chalk pencil, then remove the template and cut out the pieces. Templates in this book include a ¼-inch (6 mm) seam allowance unless otherwise stated.

Sometimes you'll need to cut out shapes in reverse. For example, the arms and legs in the flip-doll patterns are asymmetrical shapes. If you're using fabric that has a right side and a wrong side, you'll need to be sure to cut one shape in reverse, so that they will match up when you sew them together with right sides facing. This is easy enough to remember. When you're cutting out your shapes, fold your fabric in half, with right sides facing, and cut the two shapes at once. One will be in reverse. If your fabric looks the same on both sides, you won't need to worry about this; just cut out as many as needed.

MACHINE SEWING

If you're new to sewing, you may want to practice sewing straight lines. If you sew too slowly, your line may be wobbly; too fast, and you may shoot off in the wrong direction. Similarly, curves are smoother if you sew at a nice steady pace. When sewing around a corner, sew to the corner and stop with your needle down. Lift the presser foot and pivot your fabric so it's pointing in the right direction, then continue sewing. Topstitching is stitching done on the right side of the fabric to add stability or decoration to a seam. At the beginning and end of each seam, stitch backward one or two stitches on top of your seam to prevent unraveling.

TURNING

Before you turn a project right side out you need to trim corners and cut notches in the seam allowance. This helps the seam stretch a little around curves and corners so that it will lie neatly. Around curves, use small scissors to cut notches perpendicular to the seam, but make sure you don't cut through the seam. For corners that point in, cut a small slit all the way to the seam; for corners that point out, trim off the excess fabric **(figure 1)**. Just be sure you don't cut through the seam!

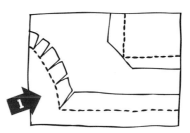

STUFFING

 To stuff a toy, add small bits of stuffing at a time, and push it to the farthest corner before adding more (using a stuffing tool if necessary; see page 12). Toys will hold their shape more neatly if you stuff firmly, so be sure to use plenty of stuffing. However, you have to be careful if the fabric has some stretch because stuffing too much may cause it to lose its shape. If you are using a weighted filling (see page 14) to stabilize the base of a toy, you can pour it in first and then add stuffing on top. However, if the toy will be moved around a lot, you may want to first sew the plastic pellets or beads into a pouch that sits in the base to prevent them from moving to other parts of the toy. Plastic beads can be quite a mess! Try using a funnel and spoon to keep the beads from spilling everywhere.

SEWING CLOSED BY HAND (LADDER STITCHING)

 Most toys will be turned right side out through a small hole that you'll need to sew closed by hand later. Be sure to leave the hole big enough to easily turn the project so that the opening doesn't get stretched or torn in the process. After the project is stuffed and you're ready to close the hole, tuck the raw edges inside and use a ladder stitch to invisibly close the opening. To make a ladder stitch, tie a knot at the end of your thread and start from the wrong side of the fabric. Make small stitches perpendicular to the seam, first on one side of the seam, then on the other, and repeat **(figure 2)**. The only part of your stitches that will be visible should look like rungs on a ladder. When you pull the thread tight the stitches will disappear.

● ●

BASTING AND TACKING

 Basting is when you sew with large stitches by hand or machine. Usually you do this to hold something together until you can stitch it in place more carefully. You can also use a basting stitch to gather fabric; after sewing the large stitches, pull the ends of the threads, gathering the fabric. Tacking can mean the same thing as basting, but it is also used as a quilting term. To tack something in place means to stitch through all the layers of fabric and tie a knot to hold them together.

SPECIAL SKILLS

ADDING TRIMS

 Depending on the project, some trims are simply topstitched (see page 17) onto the fabric as decorations. You might use twill tape as a belt or a lacy decoration on a dress. Simply position the trim where you want it, and topstitch along the center using a matching thread. If your trim is very wide, you might sew along both edges instead of in the middle.

Other trims are sewn into a seam to create a decorative edge, like the rickrack spines of the Smiling Crocodile (page 39) or the ball-trim feet on the Caterpillar (page 99). When pinning the fabric together, pin the trim in between the two layers of fabric. For rickrack, the seam should fall along the center of the rickrack so that you see one scalloped edge instead of a whole squiggly line. Ball trim is made of balls or small pompoms connected to a tape by thick threads. In this case, the seam should fall on the connecting threads so that the tape is hidden inside the seam. If you have trouble lining up your trim with the seam, try sewing the trim to one fabric first so you can see what you're doing. When you sew on the second layer, flip your stack over so that you can see where you stitched the trim, and sew on top of those stitches.

The Caterpillar and the Butterfly (page 99)

DOUBLE-FOLD BIAS TAPE

Bias tape is a neat way to finish a raw edge. It's pretty simple to sew in once you know how. First open the bias tape; notice each side is folded in, and one fold is narrower than the other. With the right sides facing, line up the narrow side to the raw edge of the fabric. Fold in the end of the tape where you will begin sewing so that the raw edge is tucked in **(figure 3a)**. Next, sew along the edge in the fold to secure the tape to the front of your project, overlapping the ends **(figure 3b)**. Fold the bias tape to the wrong side and tuck in the fold, encasing the raw edge inside the tape **(figure 3c)**. Iron the tape flat to make sure the fold is lying neatly. Turn back to the front and carefully topstitch along your previous seam, securing the back of the binding **(figure 3d)**.

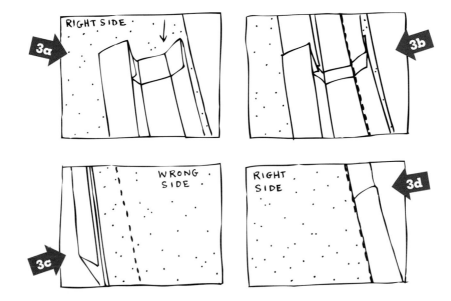

EMBROIDERY DETAILS

If you can sew by hand, you can embroider! With colorful embroidery floss and just a few simple stitches you can easily add details to your project. The embroidery floss is a bit thicker than regular sewing thread and will make your stitches stand out. You may feel comfortable embroidering freestyle, but if you're doing something very particular, like lettering, you may want to first draw your design onto the fabric using a water-soluble quilting pen or chalk pencil (see page 12), and then stitch over the drawing. This book calls for two simple stitches: backstitch and satin stitch.

A backstitch is great for anything linear, like a mouth or letters (**figure 4**).

Satin stitch is used to create a larger area of stitching, such as an eye or a mustache (**figure 5**).

APPLIQUÉ

This book only calls for felt appliqués because they're so easy. Many of these projects have lots of steps, so we take simple wherever we can get it. To make a felt appliqué, simply cut the felt to the exact shape you want—no need to worry about a seam allowance. You can stitch the appliqué directly onto the fabric using either a running stitch or a whipstitch. If you use a matching thread, stitches easily disappear in felt. A colorful embroidery floss can add decoration. If you apply the appliqué before assembling the pieces, you can also topstitch them by machine; however, hand-stitching often looks neater for tiny pieces.

A basic running stitch (**figure 6**) is sufficient for small appliqués, but be sure to use a backstitch occasionally to secure your thread.

A whipstitch wraps around the edge of the appliqué, which keeps the edge flat and looks a little more decorative (**figure 7**).

MAKING HAIR

There are two hair techniques used throughout this book that can be adapted for almost any project. The appliqué method is super simple, while the yarn method involves a few more steps but adds a more hairlike quality.

For the appliqué method, cut the hair to the exact shape from a nonfraying fabric like felt or fleece, and then appliqué it onto the doll before assembly. The back of the head can often be cut entirely from the felt with no need to appliqué anything. For the Superhero Flip Doll (page 111), I've added fleece pigtails for the girl alter ego by sewing them into the seam of the head in the same way you would sew in arms or legs. The flip dolls in this

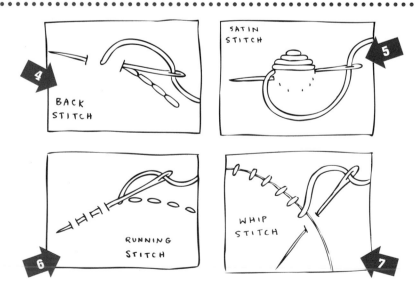

Superhero Flip Doll (page 111)

book use the appliqué method because it's fairly simple; however, you can use the yarn method if you want to.

The yarn method is a bit more complicated but works well for long hair—in this book it's used for the Winged Horse (page 60) and the Circus Flip Doll (page 120). You will create a "wig" from yarn and then sew it to the finished head by hand. Begin by cutting many equal lengths of yarn and laying them on tissue paper. Each pattern will give you specific sizes, but the idea is to cut the yarn long enough to hang down on both side of the head, so if you want hair that is about 3 inches (7.6 cm) long, you'll cut the yarn about 6 to 7 inches (15.2 to 17.8 cm) long. Once the hair is centered on the tissue paper, sew a line down the center on the sewing machine, and then stitch over it two or three more times **(figure 8a)**.

Next, tear the tissue paper away from the seam. Now you have your wig. Place it on the head of the doll and use a few pins to hold it in place. Next, hand-stitch through the wig and the head with a

matching thread along the seam to secure it **(figure 8b)**. Once the wig is attached, you may want to style the hair and stitch the hairstyle to the head in several places as well. You can also use braids or pigtails to make the hair look more natural.

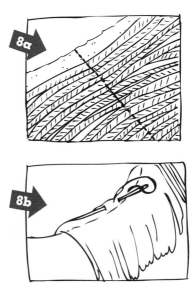

ZIPPERS

Sewing zippers is a snap with the help of a zipper foot—be sure to buy one that works with your sewing machine model. A zipper foot is skinnier than a regular presser foot, which allows you to get your needle close to the zipper teeth. Sew carefully because sewing over the zipper can break your needle. I find it helps to pin the zipper in place and sew slowly, removing the pins as I go. This helps assure that I sew a straight line, and that my zipper doesn't move out of place. Methods for sewing a zipper vary by project.

BUTTONS, BEADS, AND BUTTONHOLES

Most buttons come with two or four holes. To attach a button you simply sew through the holes several times until the button is secure, going up through one hole and down the other. I usually use four to six stitches when sewing by hand, and then knot the thread underneath the button. (Shank buttons and beads only have one hole, but they can be sewn on by hand in the same manner. Sew through the hole and then through the fabric in a circular direction and repeat four to six times.) If you are sewing a button on by machine, position the buttonhole under your presser foot with the fabric beneath. Use a zigzag stitch, and set your stitch length to 0. Adjust your stitch width until it matches the width between the two holes. To check the width, move the needle manually by turning the hand wheel

and watch how the needle lines up with the holes—don't run the machine before you're sure of the width because you may break your needle (or your button—or both)! Once the width is correct, you can sew about six stitches by machine to secure the button.

If your machine has a buttonhole feature you can simply follow the manufacturer's instructions to create a buttonhole. However, if it doesn't—or if you don't have your instructions—you can still create a buttonhole as long as you have a zig-zag stitch. A buttonhole is basically a skinny rect-angle sewn in zigzag with a hole cut in the center (**figure 9**). The zigzag stitches prevent the hole from fraying or expanding.

To make a buttonhole, first set your stitch length to 0 and make a wide stitch (about a 3). Then, move your needle to the right-hand position and change your stitch length to 1 and your stitch width to 1.5. Now sew a zigzag line slightly longer than the diameter of the button. Next, return your needle to the center position, change your stitch length to 0 and your width to 3, and sew another wide zigzag as before. Then move the needle to the left-hand position, change the stitch length to 1 and the width to 1.5, and sew in reverse back to where you started, completing the rectangle. Carefully snip a straight line with small, sharp scissors in the center of your stitches—don't cut through your stitching! If you do accidentally cut through your stitches (it happens), simply zigzag over the cut to recreate your stitches. Ta da!

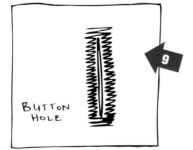

Sly Fox (page 43)

customizing flip dolls

Traditional topsy-turvy dolls hide one character under the skirt of the other, but my version of the flip doll hides one character inside of the other. This means the upper body shapes can vary quite a bit, allowing you to make girls, boys, or animals in the same doll. If you look closely at the patterns for George and the Dragon (page 102), the Owl and the Pussycat (page 108), the Super-hero Flip Doll (page 111), and the Vampire and Bat (page 116), you'll notice they all use a very similar pattern. By using this basic shape, you can customize my pattern to make characters from many of your favorite stories. Here are a few tips to get you started.

THE BASIC SHAPE

Figure 10 shows the basic flip doll pattern. Your two dolls should be the same height and the same width at the base. They will usually share a pair of legs. Also, I usually give them a neck at the same place, but this isn't strictly necessary. However, the more closely the two doll shapes resemble one another, the more nicely the finished doll will fill out.

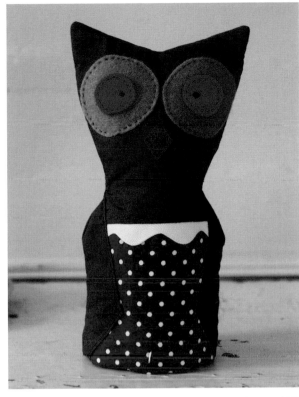

The Owl and the Pussycat (page 108)

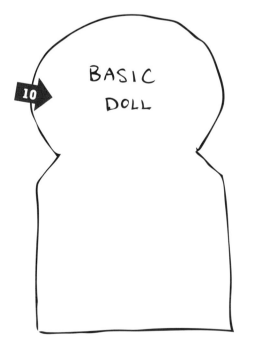

BASIC DOLL

The History of Flip Dolls

Topsy-turvy dolls have a rich history in America. Before the Civil War, black/white dolls were common. Historians disagree about the exact motive for making these biracial, two-headed dolls; however, they clearly reflected the racial conflicts and divisions of the time. The dolls—emblems of the era's tensions—allowed children to explore serious issues in a nonthreatening way.

After the Civil War, more styles of topsy-turvy dolls became popular, including storybook dolls. The most common doll featured Little Red Riding Hood on one side, and the grandmother and the wolf on the other. There were also sleeping/awake, happy/sad, and rich/poor dolls. These types of dolls are loaded with potential for children to explore identity, opposites, transformation, and storytelling.

THE VARIATIONS

Of course, you want the two dolls to be different! You can change the shape of the head, as long as it fits within the basic shape and the height of the dolls remains the same. You can also change the shape of the body as long as it doesn't vary too much from the main shape and the base stays the same. Sew ears, arms, tails, or any other appendage into the seams because they will fold in and not affect the shape of the doll. Appliqué or embroider decorations and facial features to help identify your characters. Some examples of variations can be seen in **figure 11**.

THE ASSEMBLY

Every flip doll in this book is made in the same way: you create each half of the doll separately. First make one doll by assembling the pieces for the front, then the back, and then the appendages. Sew them all together with a layer of batting, and add appliqué and embroidery as desired. Repeat with the second doll, leaving an opening for turning in the side. Put one doll inside the other and sew them together at the waist. Anchor the heads together, then turn them right side out and finish.

RAG DOLLS

All of the dolls from these patterns can be made as rag dolls, too. Rag dolls are also great for storytelling or for small children to use in acting out stories. To use these patterns to make rag dolls, you'll need to make two simple changes: cut four legs for each doll instead of two because they will no longer share a pair of legs. Make and attach the legs in the same way as before.

When you assemble the dolls, sew the bottom of the doll closed like all of the other sides. Leave an opening in the side of each doll to turn it right side out. Stuff it firmly, then close the opening with a ladder stitch.

Vampire and Bat (page 116)

ZIP & STACK

The patterns in this section are great for beginners because they use very basic forms with some fun embellishments. The Stacking Trees, Nesting Flowers, and Elephant Parade have multiple pieces that can be assembled in various ways, making them easy to sew but full of play potential. Smiling Crocodile and Sly Fox are some of my favorite toys! They use simple animal shapes with a fun zipper mouth that is sure to make you smile, too. (And speaking of smiles, the Chesire Cat has a unique one as well!)

Stacking Trees

Bring back the beanbag! These versatile triangles can be arranged in myriad ways to create a single tree or a whole forest. Make multiple sets to create your own little woodland or one very tall tree. Go hunting for a variety of green prints and textures to make your forest diverse.

DIFFICULTY → ← EASY

- -

⚡ TOOLS & MATERIALS

Basic Sewing Tool Kit (page 10)
Stacking Trees template (page 124)
8 x 8-inch (20.3 x 20.3 cm) pieces (or less) of 6 different green fabrics in various textures and prints

Threads to match fabrics
Weighted filling (page 14)
Funnel and spoon (for adding the weighted filling)

- -

⚡ INSTRUCTIONS

1 Copy the templates and cut them out.

2 Cut out two of each triangular Tree size and one Topper rectangle, using a different fabric for each pair of triangles and for the topper.

3 With right sides facing, sew each pair of triangles together, leaving a 1-inch (2.5 cm) opening to turn them right side out.

4 To sew the tree topper, fold the rectangle in half crosswise and sew along the top and side edges, leaving a 1-inch (2.5 cm) opening on the side **(figure 1a)**. Next, squash the unsewn edge so that the side seam lies on top of what was the folded edge **(figure 1b)**. Sew the bottom edge closed.

- -

5 Clip all of the corners and turn each tree right side out through the openings. Poke the corners out carefully with a chopstick or other turning tool.

6 Fill the bags with weighted filling using a funnel and spoon. Leave enough empty space so that the bag is full but flexible.

7 Once each bag is full, stitch the opening closed using a ladder stitch. Go over the opening twice to make it secure.

Stack and enjoy!

Nesting Flowers

These flowers are a twist on the popular preschool nesting cups, with petals and leaves stacking and nesting to form the flower. Nest all the pieces to make a pretty poppy, or take them apart to make four smaller flowers. Try this in different colors to make a daisy, rose, or your favorite flower.

DIFFICULTY — **MODERATE**

⚡ TOOLS & MATERIALS

Basic Sewing Tool Kit (page 10)

Nesting Flowers template (page 124)

9 x 12-inch (22.9 x 30.5 cm) piece of red fabric for the XL flower

7 x 10-inch (17.8 x 25.4 cm) piece of dark pink fabric for the L flower

6 x 8-inch (15.2 x 20.3 cm) piece of pink fabric for the M flower

3½ x 5-inch (8.9 x 12.7 cm) piece of peach fabric for the S flower

3 x 2-inch (7.6 x 5.1 cm) piece of yellow fabric for the pistil

8 x 12-inch (20.3 x 30.5 cm) piece of green fabric for the calyx

8 x 6-inch (20.3 x 15.2 cm) piece of light green fabric for the L leaf

6 x 6-inch (15.2 x 15.2 cm) piece of green fabric for the M leaf

6 x 4-inch (15.2 x 10.2 cm) piece of dark green fabric for the S leaf

¼ yard (22.9 cm) of batting

¼ yard (22.9 cm) of fusible interfacing

Threads to match fabrics

Stuffing

⚡ INSTRUCTIONS

1 Copy the templates and cut them out.

2 Cut out four Flowers of each size in their respective fabric colors, and cut two pieces of batting for each size. Cut two yellow Pistils. Cut two green Calyxes and one piece of batting. Cut two Leaves of each size from light green, green, or dark green fabric, and one piece of batting for each size also.

3 To make the leaves and calyx, stack each pair of leaves with right sides facing and place the batting on the bottom of the stack. Sew around each leaf, securing all three layers and leaving a 1½-inch (3.8 cm) opening in each one. Clip slits in the seam allowance, paying special attention to the corners, and turn each one right side out. Iron each leaf flat and hand-sew the opening closed using a ladder stitch.

4 Assemble the flowers. Stack two flower pieces of the same size with right sides facing and place a layer of batting on the bottom of the stack. Sew around the flower, leaving the bottom open between the two dots on the template. Repeat with the other two flower pieces of the same size. Clip slits in the seam allowance and turn them right side out. Iron each flower flat.

5 Stack the two halves of the flower on top of one another. Fold back the outer layers on the bottom. Sew the two inner layers together from one dot to the other **(figure 1)**.

6 Now turn the entire flower wrong side out again. Sew the bottom outer edges together from dot to dot, leaving a 1½-inch (3.8 cm) opening in the center. Be careful not to sew through the other layers **(figure 2)**.

7 Turn the flower right side out again. Iron flat and sew the opening closed with a ladder stitch. Repeat steps 4 through 7 for each size of flower.

8 To make the pistil, sew the two shapes together with right sides facing, leaving the bottom open. Clip slits in the seam allowance and turn right side out.

9 Fold in the pistil's bottom edge about ¼ inch (6 mm) and iron the fold to crease. Open it again, and stuff the pistil firmly. Squash the bottom folded edge closed the opposite way so that the side seam is in the center instead of the side. This will create a wider bottom for the pistil to sit on. Sew the bottom edge closed using a ladder stitch.

Now you're ready to nest!

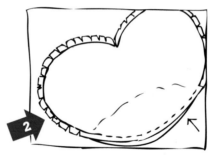

Elephant Parade

This herd of elephants may surprise you. Hook them trunk to tail and stand them in a circle or hang them on the wall as elephant bunting.

SPECIAL SKILLS »» Appliqué (page 20)

✎ TOOLS & MATERIALS

Basic Sewing Tool Kit (page 10)
Elephant Parade template (page 125)
12 x 14-inch (30.5 x 35.6 cm) pieces of
  6 different fabrics in various textures
  and prints in blues, purples, or grays

8 x 10-inch (20.3 x 25.4 cm) pieces of felt
  in coordinating colors
Thread to match fabrics and felt
Stuffing
Pinking shears

✎ INSTRUCTIONS

1 Copy the template and cut it out.

2 Trace and cut out two elephant Bodies (one in reverse) from each fabric.

3 Trace and cut out two Ears from felt for each elephant.

4 With wrong sides facing, sew each pair of matching elephants together, leaving a 1-inch (2.5 cm) opening on the elephant's back.

5 Trim the seam allowance with pinking shears, being careful not to cut through the stitches.

6 Stuff each elephant very firmly, then stitch over the opening twice to close it securely.

7 Use a whipstitch with matching thread to sew a felt ear to each side of the elephant's body. Repeat this step for each elephant.

Hey, a herd of elephants!

Cheshire Cat

This Cheshire Cat uses high-tech flannel graph technology to try on a variety of expressions. His weighted bottom helps him sit still while you play with him, which makes him a good fit for a windowsill or desk.

DIFFICULTY ◄ ► MODERATE

SPECIAL SKILLS »» Embroidery Details (page 20) »» Buttons, Beads, and Buttonholes (page 22)

✎ TOOLS & MATERIALS

Basic Sewing Tool Kit (page 10)
Cheshire Cat template (page 125)
24 x 12-inch (61 x 30.5 cm) piece of fleece, flannel, or felt
Thread to match fabric, plus black and white
Weighted filling (page 14)

Funnel and spoon (for adding the weighted filling)
Stuffing
Embroidery floss for the eyes and nose
A few sheets of white, black, and red craft felt for the mouth and mustache shapes
8 x 10-inch (20.3 x 25.4 cm) piece of fusible interfacing
2 medium buttons for the eyes

✎ INSTRUCTIONS

1 Copy the templates and cut them out.

2 Cut out two Bodies (one in reverse), one Gusset, one Pocket, and two Tails.

3 With right sides facing, sew the two tails together, leaving the end open. Clip slits in the seam allowance and turn it right side out. Using the funnel and spoon, fill the tail with weighted filling, pin it closed, and set it aside.

4 Hem the top edge of the pocket by folding it twice, hiding the raw edge, and topstitch on the fold. Pin the pocket to the back body piece with the other three edges turned under by a ¼ inch (6 mm). Secure the pocket by topstitching those three edges to the body.

5 Sew one edge of the bottom gusset to the bottom edge of the front body piece. Repeat, this time sewing the other gusset edge to the back body piece.

6 Line up the edges of the body pieces and pin them together. Pin the tail in the seam near the cat's bottom. Sew the front and back together, leaving a 2-inch (5.1 cm) opening along the back and securing the tail in the seam.

7 Clip small slits in all of the seam allowances, especially around corners and curves. Turn the cat right side out.

8 Pour ½ cup (125 g) of weighted filling into the bottom of the cat, then stuff the rest of the body firmly with polyester fiberfill. Sew the opening closed using a ladder stitch.

9 Stitch the buttons on for the eyes using black embroidery floss. Embroider the nose with a backstitch.

10 With a water-soluble quilting pen, draw the mouth shapes onto white felt, the lips on red felt, and a mustache on black felt. Cut out the block of felt around the shapes, not the shapes themselves. With black thread, topstitch the lines of the teeth on the white felt. Switch to white thread and stitch around the perimeter of the mouths. This will secure your black thread when you cut out the mouths. You won't need to topstitch on the red lips or black mustaches, but still cut out a block around the shape. Do not cut out the shapes too early! It will be much easier to do the topstitching and fuse the interfacing with a large block of felt.

11 Follow the manufacturer's instructions to fuse the interfacing to the back of the felt. If you are using acrylic craft felt, be sure to put a layer of fabric between your felt and the iron so that you don't burn it. The interfacing will secure and hide your stitches on the back, and it will also make your shapes stick to the cat's body.

12 Carefully cut out the mouth and mustache shapes. Stick on a mouth to suit your mood, and tuck the rest in the cat's back pocket for later!

NOTE: Try drawing some of your own mouth shapes, too! Or what about villainous eyebrows, vampire teeth, or a beauty spot? Felt is easy to cut and use, and it comes in many colors—use this method to create any accessory you can imagine.

Smiling Crocodile

Watch out for this toothy grin—he bites! Smiling Crocodiles make fun toys for little hands learning to zip and unzip. Enlarge the pattern and make a quirky throw pillow. Use a chunky brass zipper for gold teeth or a dainty pink zipper for a pleasant smile. Once you get the hang of this pattern, try drawing your own toothy animal: a shark, dinosaur, or wolf!

DIFFICULTY **MODERATE**

SPECIAL SKILLS » Adding Trims (page 18) » Embroidery Details (page 20) » Zippers (page 22)
Optional: Buttons, Beads, and Buttonholes (page 22)

⚡ TOOLS & MATERIALS

Basic Sewing Tool Kit (page 10)

Smiling Crocodile template (page 126)

14 x 12-inch (35.6 x 30.5 cm) piece of green fabric*

10-inch (25.4 cm) length of medium rickrack*

Threads to match fabric

Scrap of fusible interfacing (optional)

7-inch (17.8 cm) zipper*

Zipper foot

Stuffing

Embroidery floss for the eyes

* For larger crocodiles (25 inches [63.5 cm] long), you will use these instead:

28 x 24-inch (71 x 60.1 cm) piece of green fabric

20-inch (50.8 cm) length of jumbo rickrack

10-inch (25.4 cm) zipper

2 large buttons for the eyes (optional)

NOTE: A fabric with a little stretch, like fleece or flannel, will make sewing the zipper mouth easier, but you can use any medium- to heavyweight fabric.

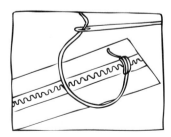

NOTE: Your zipper should be a little bit longer than the sewn mouth area. If you have a zipper that is too long, you can easily shorten it to fit. With the zipper zipped, make a few whipstitches around the teeth of the zipper at the correct length. Then trim the zipper behind the stitches.

⚡ INSTRUCTIONS

1 Copy the template and cut it out.

2 Cut out two Bodies, one in reverse.

3 Pin the bodies together with the rickrack sandwiched between, from the back of the head to the tip of the tail. Pin the center-line of the rickrack where the seam will be sewn, so that half of the rickrack is on the outside and half is unseen inside. (To make sure your rickrack doesn't shift, you can sew it to one side before sewing all three layers together.) Sew the bodies together, leaving a 2-inch (5.1 cm) opening in the tail.

4 Clip slits in the seam allowance, especially in the corners and around curves. Be sure not to cut into the seam! Turn right side out to make sure everything is sewn neatly.

5 Turn wrong side out again and cut the mouth opening as indicated on the template, cutting a tiny Y on the end. If you are using a thin fabric or one that frays easily, you may want to stabilize the fabric around the mouth with fusible interfacing before cutting the mouth open.

6 To sew in the zipper, first unzip the zipper and lay it on top of the opening. Next, flip the teeth on the top half of the zipper toward the top of the crocodile and pin the zipper between the two layers of the mouth **(figure 1a)**. Then flip the teeth on the bottom half of the zipper toward the bottom of the crocodile and pin the bottom of the zipper in place. The zipper should be twisting outward in both directions **(figure 1b)**. Now, tuck the twisted end of the zipper inside the crocodile at the Y so that the fabric will lie flat.

7 Use a zipper foot to sew the zipper into the mouth on the top first, then the bottom. Sew all the way to the points of the Y, but do not sew around the end.

8 Turn the crocodile right side out, pulling gently on the zipper to push the nose out. Use a chopstick or other turning tool to help push out all the points. Tuck the end of the zipper inside the body—the corner of the mouth is still unfinished for now.

9 Stuff the crocodile. Use small bits to first stuff the mouth, pushing it all the way to the end with a chopstick or other tool. Be sure to put stuffing all around the end of the zipper so it isn't pressed against either side. Stuff the body firmly and hand-sew the opening in the tail closed using a ladder stitch.

10 Now tuck in the point of the Y at the end of the mouth and sew that small opening closed. Use a ladder stitch to sew the opening closed on one side of the face. Then sew the other side, making your stitches line up with the stitches from the other side so that they don't show **(figure 2)**.

11 Embroider an eye on each side using a satin stitch. For larger crocodiles you may want to use button eyes.

Love that smile, Crocodile!

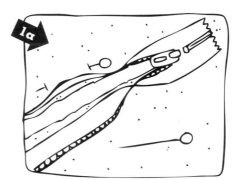

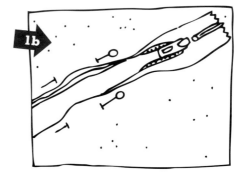

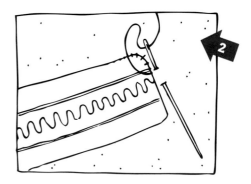

Sly Fox

This fox is another fun zipper-mouth toy in a large pillow size. Unzip his smile to feel his sharp teeth, but be sure to zip him up before you go to sleep. He's guaranteed to bring a sly grin to anyone's face.

DIFFICULTY — MODERATE

SPECIAL SKILLS »» Zippers (page 22) »» Buttons, Beads, and Buttonholes (page 22)

⚡ TOOLS & MATERIALS

Basic Sewing Tool Kit (page 10)

Sly Fox template (page 127)

36 x 20-inch (76.2 x 50.8 cm) piece of orange fleece or flannel

10 x 5-inch (25.4 x 12.7 cm) piece of white fleece or flannel

Threads to match fabrics

Scrap of fusible interfacing (optional)

9-inch (22.9 cm) white zipper

Zipper foot

Stuffing

2 large white buttons

Black embroidery floss for the eyes

NOTE: A fabric with a little stretch, like fleece or flannel, will make sewing the zipper mouth easier, but you can use any medium- to heavy-weight fabric.

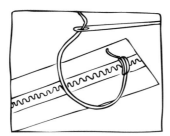

NOTE: Your zipper should be a little bit longer than the sewn mouth area. If you have a zipper that is too long, you can easily shorten it to fit. With the zipper zipped, make a few whipstitches around the teeth of the zipper at the correct length. Then trim the zipper behind the stitches.

⚡ INSTRUCTIONS

1 Copy the templates and cut them out.

2 Cut out two fox Bodies (one in reverse) from the orange fabric and two Tail tips (one in reverse) from the white fabric, adding a ¼-inch (6 mm) seam allowance to the flat side of the Tail tip. Sew the white tails onto the bodies.

3 Pin and sew the bodies together, right sides facing, leaving a 2-inch (5.1 cm) opening on the bottom edge.

4 Clip slits in the seam allowance, especially in corners and around curves. Be sure not to cut into the seam! Turn right side out to make sure everything is sewn neatly.

5 Turn wrong side out again and cut the mouth opening as indicated on the template, cutting a tiny Y on the end as shown on the template. If you are using a thin fabric or one that frays easily, you may want to stabilize the fabric around the mouth with fusible interfacing before cutting the mouth open.

6 To sew in the zipper, first unzip the zipper and lay it on top of the opening. Next, flip the teeth on the top half of the zipper toward the top of the fox and pin the zipper between the two layers of the mouth **(figure 1a)**. Then flip the teeth on the bottom half of the zipper toward the bottom of the fox and pin the bottom of the zipper in place. Your zipper should be twisting outward in both directions **(figure 1b)**. Now tuck the twisted end of the zipper inside the fox at the Y.

7 Using a zipper foot, sew the zipper into the mouth on the top and then the bottom. Sew all the way to the points of the Y, but do not sew around the end.

8 Turn the fox right side out. Use a chopstick or other turning tool to help push all the points out, if needed. When it is fully turned, tuck the end of the zipper inside the opening at the inside end of the mouth. The corner of the mouth is left unfinished for now.

9 Use small bits of stuffing to stuff the mouth, pushing it all the way into the point with a chopstick or other tool. Be sure to put stuffing all around the end of the zipper so it isn't pressed against either side. Stuff the body firmly and sew the opening on the bottom by hand using a ladder stitch.

10 Now tuck in the point of the Y at the end of the mouth and sew that small opening closed. Use a ladder stitch to sew the opening closed on one side of the face. Then sew the other side, making your stitches line up with the stitches from the other side so that they don't show **(figure 2)**.

11 Sew on the button eyes using a white button and black embroidery floss.

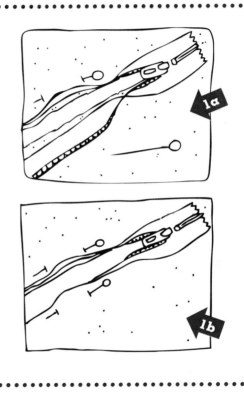

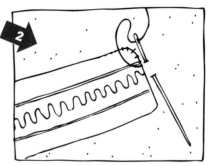

HIDE, SEEK, & GO!

The toys in this section rely on these three elementary forms of play; they are all about discovery and motion. Gulp the Whale is a plush toy with a deep stomach where you can tuck a treasure. Hide surprises inside your Nuts 'n Bolts Robot, then look for them through the vinyl window. Peekaboo Turtle slips in and out of her shell, ready to crawl or hide. The Getaway Car uses a button joint for the wheel axle so that all four wheels turn. The wings of the Winged Horse pivot on the buttons to help him fly—or they unbutton entirely when he wants to blend in. Spring the Bouncy Bunny by the elastic loop and watch her weighted legs jump up and down.

Peekaboo Turtle

Your little turtle comes out of her shell to say hello! Make a few extra shells for your turtle—even reptiles need options.

DIFFICULTY → ← MODERATE

SPECIAL SKILLS ⟫ Embroidery Details (page 20)

✎ TOOLS & MATERIALS

Basic Sewing Tool Kit (page 10)

Peekaboo Turtle template (page 128)

11 x 14-inch (27.9 x 35.6 cm) piece of fabric for the body

12 x 16-inch (30.5 x 40.6 cm) piece of fabric for the inner shell

12 x 16-inch (30.5 x 40.6 cm) piece of fabric for the outer shell

8 x 14-inch (20.3 x 35.6 cm) piece of low-loft batting (see page 14; I prefer the softness of cotton batting for this project)

Threads to match fabrics

Stuffing

Embroidery floss for the eyes

✎ INSTRUCTIONS

1 Copy the templates and cut them out.

2 Cut one of each Body template (Top and Bottom) in the body fabric, a Shell Top and Bottom from the inner shell fabric, and a Shell Top and Bottom from the outer shell fabric. Cut two low-loft batting pieces from the Bottom Shell template.

3 Stack the two Shell Bottom pieces with right sides facing on top of one piece of batting. Sew the layers, leaving a 1-inch (2.5 cm) opening. Clip slits in the seam allowance and turn right side out through the opening.

Iron so that the edges of the opening are folded in. Topstitch around the edge, closing the opening as you go.

4 Sew the darts in the Shell Top pieces one at a time (these darts will add shape to the shell). Fold the fabric along the light gray lines and sew from the inside to the outer edge for each of the eight darts.

5 Stack the two shell top pieces, right sides facing, on the remaining batting, lining up the dart seams. Sew around the edge, leaving a small opening to turn the piece right side out. Clip slits in the seam allowance and turn right side out. Iron the shell, then topstitch around the edge, closing the opening as you go.

6 Tack the shell top to the shell bottom where indicated by black dots on the template. Make four strong tacking stitches in the topstitching on each dot.

7 Create the round head on the top body piece by pinning the curved edge A to the straight edge B of the turtle's head. Sew edge A to edge B (or align the fabrics as you sew without pinning them first). Repeat on the other side of the head, sewing the straight edge C to the curved edge D.

8 Pin the top body to the bottom body with right sides facing, carefully lining up the newly sewn edges of the top head with the bottom head. Sew the top to the bottom, leaving a small opening in the hind leg. Clip small slits all the way around the body in the seam allowance right up to the seam. Take your time! Be careful not to cut through the seam, and pay special attention to sharp corners.

9 Turn the body right side out and poke out all points with a chopstick or other turning tool. Stuff the body firmly, adding small amounts of stuffing at a time. Sew the opening closed by hand using a ladder stitch.

10 Embroider the eyes using a satin stitch.

11 Slip the turtle body into the turtle shell with the tacked points of the shell tucked in between the front and hind legs.

Now slip the turtle into a different shell. Maybe something with a stripe? What can I say? She's fickle!

Getaway Car

Getaway Car

Every car needs a nice set of wheels! Button joints work nicely as tire axles on this simple little design. Find shiny buttons for flashy hubcaps, use a racing stripe print, or go with a classic red fabric. How do you roll?

SPECIAL SKILLS ⟫ Buttons, Beads, and Buttonholes (page 22)

✎ TOOLS & MATERIALS

Basic Sewing Tool Kit (page 10)

Getaway Car template (page 129)

8 x 8-inch (20.3 x 20.3 cm) piece of fabric for the body

12 x 12-inch (30.5 x 30.5 cm) piece of fabric for the wheels

1½ x 28-inch (3.8 x 71.1 cm) strip of fabric for the body

Thread to match the fabrics, plus black

Stuffing

4 medium buttons

✎ INSTRUCTIONS

1 Copy the templates and cut them out.

2 From the body fabric, cut two car Bodies.

3 From the wheel fabric, cut eight Wheels. Sew two wheel pieces together with right sides facing, leaving an opening to turn. Clip slits in the seam allowance and turn the wheel right side out. Repeat three times to make four wheels. Stuff the wheels firmly and sew them closed by hand using a ladder stitch.

4 Fold in the end of the long strip of fabric about 1 inch (2.5 cm) from one end and iron it flat. Start at the fold and sew the long strip around the perimeter of one side of the car, following the curves carefully. Leave 1 inch (2.5 cm) at the end of the strip. Sew the opposite side of the long strip to the other side of the car. Be sure to start sewing the strip in the same direction as on the first side so that it doesn't pull unevenly. Your ends should overlap in the seam allowance **(figure 1)**.

5 Clip slits carefully in the seam allowance, especially around the curves. Turn the car right side out through the opening in the side and stuff it firmly. Sew the opening closed with a ladder stitch.

6 Add the wheels using a button joint. Thread a large needle with black thread, and tie the ends together in a knot so that the thread is doubled. Make a stitch in the center of one wheel from the wrong side or back of the wheel, securing the thread, then insert the needle through two holes of a button and back through the wheel, fixing the button to the outside of the wheel. Insert the needle straight through the car, coming out on the opposite side. Then push the needle through the center of another wheel and through a second button. Pull the thread taut so that the wheels are firmly in place. Then pass the needle back through the car to the first side again, repeating the sequence: wheel, button, wheel, car, wheel, button, wheel, and back in the car. Pull tight and repeat several times until the wheels and buttons are securely attached **(figure 2)**. Tie off the thread behind one button and trim the ends. Repeat for the other set of wheels.

Now you're ready to roll!

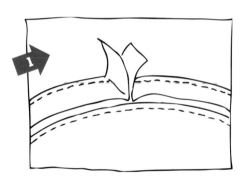

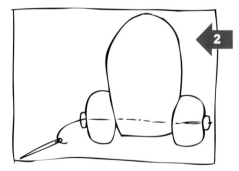

Bouncy Bunny

This bunny has big floppy ears and long floppy weighted feet. Bounce her by the elastic loop on her back and watch her legs jump!

✎ TOOLS & MATERIALS

Basic Sewing Tool Kit (page 10)

Bouncy Bunny template (page 129)

35 x 10-inch (88.9 x 25.4 cm) piece of fabric for the body

12 x 10-inch (30.5 x 25.4 cm) piece of accent fabric for the tummy and inner ears

Thread to match the fabrics

6 inches (15.2 cm) of elastic cord

Weighted filling (page 14)

Funnel and spoon (for adding the weighted filling)

Stuffing

Embroidery floss for the eyes

2 yards (1.8 m) of fluffy white yarn for the tail

✎ INSTRUCTIONS

1 Copy the templates and cut them out.

2 Cut out two Bodies (one in reverse), four Legs (two in reverse), two Ears, and one Head Gusset from the body fabric. Cut two Tummy Gussets (one in reverse) and two Ears from the accent fabric.

3 With right sides facing, sew the tummy gussets together along the long edge, leaving a 1½-inch (3.8 cm) opening in the center.

4 Sew the left tummy gusset to the left body piece with right sides facing, starting where you joined the tummy gussets in the front, continuing around the arms, and ending at the bottom of the gusset seam. Repeat with the other side. Be sure not to sew past the seam in the gusset for the neatest results **(figure 1)**.

5 Cut holes in the two inner leg pieces and on the body pieces where shown on the template. With right sides facing, line up the holes and be sure to position the legs at the desired angle (the feet should be pointing down). Sew around the holes with a ¼-inch (6 mm) seam allowance. Repeat with the opposite leg.

6 Push each leg through the hole to the wrong side of the body. Pin the outer leg to the inner leg with right sides facing and sew them together, moving the body out of the way of the sewing machine as you go. Repeat with the opposite leg.

7 Sew the ears together so that each one has the body fabric on the outside and the accent fabric on the inside. Clip slits in the seam allowance and turn them right side out. Pinch the ear in half at the base and iron to crease the fold.

8 Pin the head gusset to the top of the head on one side of the body with the point at the nose. Insert the folded ear into the seam—make sure the inside of the ear (with the accent fabric) is facing forward! Sew from the nose to the opposite point, leaving a little seam allowance at each point **(figure 1)**. Repeat on the opposite side of the head. Be sure to position the ears evenly.

9 Sew from the nose down the chest. Do not sew past the gusset into the seam allowance.

10 Fold 6 inches (7.6 cm) of elastic cord in half into a 3-inch loop and insert the ends into the seam at the base of the neck. Sew from the head gusset down the back to the tummy gusset, backstitching over the elastic cord to secure it.

11 Carefully clip slits in the seam allowances of the body, the legs, and the leg joints. Turn the bunny right side out through the tummy opening.

12 To stuff the body, first pour weighted filling into the feet using a funnel and spoon. Don't fill the whole leg; a little empty space allows the feet to move more freely. Stuff the top of the legs with regular stuffing to fill out the shape of the haunches and to keep the pellets from falling out of the legs. Stuff the rest of the body firmly and sew the tummy closed using a ladder stitch.

13 Embroider the eye where shown on the template using contrasting embroidery floss and a satin stitch.

14 To make the tail, wind the fluffy white yarn around four fingers **(figure 2a)**. How much yarn you use depends on the weight of your yarn; keep winding until it looks full enough for a bunny tail. When you are satisfied with the thickness, cut the yarn. Pass the cut end of the yarn between your middle two fingers and tie it around the center of the yarn **(figure 2b)**. Trim the yarn and slip your fingers out. Now use thread to stitch the tail to the bunny's rump with about a dozen strong stitches. Tie a knot and trim your thread.

Now you're hopping!

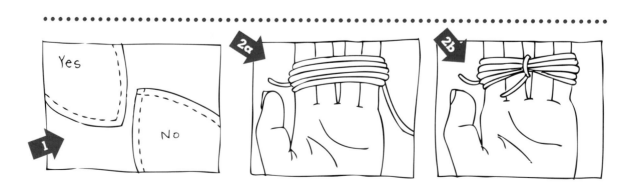

Gulp the Whale

Gulp the Whale

Some whales swim with their mouths open to catch their food, but sometimes they catch more than just food. This whale has a deep, deep stomach—perfect for hiding treasure! The pouch is big enough to hold a wallet or cell phone, a pocket diary, or a diamond ring. What will your whale hide?

DIFFICULTY — MODERATE

SPECIAL SKILLS »» Appliqué (page 20) »» Embroidery Details (page 20)

✎ TOOLS & MATERIALS

Basic Sewing Tool Kit (page 10)

Gulp the Whale template (page 130)

15 x 12-inch (38.1 x 30.5 cm) piece of blue fabric for the body

5 x 7-inch (12.7 x 17.8 cm) piece of accent fabric for the bottom gusset (underbelly)

10 x 8-inch (25.4 x 20.3 cm) piece of pink fabric for the stomach

2 x 4-inch (5.1 x 10.2 cm) piece of white felt

Thread to match the fabrics

Stuffing

Embroidery floss for the eyes

✎ INSTRUCTIONS

1 Copy the templates and cut them out.

2 Cut out two Bodies (reversing one) and one Top Gusset from the blue fabric. Cut one Bottom Gusset from the accent fabric. Cut two Stomachs from the pink fabric. Cut two Eyes from white felt.

3 With right sides facing, pin the top gusset to the left body with the wide part of the gusset in the front and the point going toward the tail. Sew them together from the front of the head along the back.

Then sew the gusset to the right body in the same manner.

4 Finish sewing the bodies together along the top and around the tail.

5 With right sides facing, sew the two stomachs together along the short, straight end.

6 With right sides facing, sew one end of the stomach to the wide end of the bottom gusset. Sew the opposite end of the stomach to the wide end of the top gusset. Make sure the seam allowances are all on the wrong side!

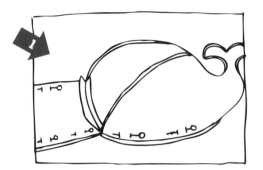

10 Pin the eyes onto the whale body, making sure they're even. Appliqué them to the body with a whipstitch. Tuck a little bit of stuffing under each eye before finishing your stitches to give them some shape. Embroider a small black circle on each eye using a satin stitch.

Your whale is ready to go, and he's hungry!

7 Turn the top of the whale inside out with the pink stomach sticking out in front of the whale. Fold the stomach in half along the short seamed end and line up the sides of the stomach. Pin the bottom gusset to the whale body, and pin the sides of the stomach together **(figure 1)**. Starting at the folded edge of the stomach, sew the left side of the stomach closed and continue, sewing the bottom gusset to the body. Repeat on the right side, leaving a 2-inch (5.1 cm) opening in the side of the stomach near the mouth for turning.

8 Clip slits in the seam allowances, paying special attention to the corners around the tail and mouth. Turn the whale right side out.

9 Stuff the whale firmly through the opening in the stomach/mouth area. The stomach should still be outside of the body—and don't stuff the stomach! When the whale is fully stuffed, push the stomach into the whale in the middle of all the stuffing. Spread it out so that it lies flat inside.

Winged Horse

The wings on this Pegasus pivot on buttons, so you can flap them or pose them any way you like. And when he's tired from a long day and just wants to blend in? Unbutton his wings so he can be an ordinary horse.

DIFFICULTY   MODERATE

SPECIAL SKILLS »» Embroidery Details (page 20) »» Making Hair (page 20)
Buttons, Beads, and Buttonholes (page 22)

⚡ TOOLS & MATERIALS

Basic Sewing Tool Kit (page 10)

Winged Horse template (page 131)

32 x 10-inch (81.3 x 25.4 cm) piece of fabric for the body

14 x 14-inch (35.6 x 35.6 cm) piece of fabric for the wings

7 x 7-inch (17.8 x 17.8 cm) piece of batting for the wings

Thread to match the fabrics and for topstitching

Stuffing

Black embroidery floss for the eyes

Yarn

Tissue paper

2 small buttons the same color as the horse's body

⚡ INSTRUCTIONS

1 Copy the templates and cut them out.

2 Cut out two Bodies (one in reverse), two Gussets (one in reverse), and two Ears from the body fabric. Cut out two Ears and four Wings (two in reverse) from the wing fabric. Cut out two Wings from the batting.

3 With right sides facing, sew the tummy gussets together along the long edge, leaving a 1½-inch (3.8 cm) opening in the middle.

4 Open the tummy gusset, and fold each leg in toward the tummy with right sides together, where indicated on the pattern. With a leg folded in, sew a curved line from one side to the other, but don't sew within the seam allowance (**figure 1**). The outside shape of the legs will be the same as before; this "dart" helps keep the legs from splaying out. Repeat on each leg.

5 Sew the left tummy gusset to the left body with right sides facing, starting where you joined the tummy gussets in the front, around the legs, and ending at the opposite seam. Repeat with the opposite side.

6 Finish sewing around the edges of the body, from the chest to the tail end.

7 Clip small slits all the way around the body in the seam allowance right up to the seam, being careful not to cut through the seam. Turn the body right side out and poke out all points with a chopstick or another blunt turning tool. Make sure all the seams are sewn neatly and make any repairs now.

8 Sew one ear cut from the main body fabric and one cut from the wing fabric with right sides facing, leaving the bottom open. Clip slits in the curve and turn the ear right side out. Repeat with the other ear. Iron the ears flat so that the edges look neat, then fold the ears in half, with the accent fabric on the inside, and iron again to crease them. Cut the bottom edge of the ear at an angle as shown on the template.

9 Carefully cut through both sides of the head along the straight gray line on the template. Turn the body wrong side out. (It isn't necessary to completely turn the legs wrong side out again, just turn them enough so that you can comfortably work with the head.) Insert the ears into the opening on top of the head with the inner ear facing out. Pin the ears in place on each side. Carefully sew the opening closed.

10 Turn the body right side out. Check the ears for neatness and make adjustments if necessary. Stuff firmly and sew the tummy closed using a ladder stitch.

11 Embroider the eyes with black embroidery floss using a satin stitch.

12 Cut 3 to 4 dozen 4-inch (10.2 cm) lengths of yarn and lay them on a sheet of tissue paper in a row about 4 inches (10.2 cm) wide. The more yarn you use, the bushier the horse's mane will be. Sew down the center of your stack of yarn twice to secure it (**figure 2**). Once sewn, tear away the tissue paper and you will have a horse wig. Center the wig on the horse's head and neck and stitch it in place along the neck seam. Stitch over it several times to secure it (**figure 3**).

13 Use the same method to create the tail. Cut about a dozen 6-inch (15.2 cm) lengths of yarn and lay them on the tissue paper no more than 1 inch (2.5 cm) wide. Stitch over the center, and tear away the tissue paper. Fold the yarn in half at the seam, and stitch the seam to the horse's tail end securely by hand.

14 Stack the wings together with right sides facing and one layer of batting on the bottom. Sew through all layers, leaving a 1½-inch (3.8 cm) opening along a flat edge. Turn the wing right side out and iron the wing, turning in the raw edges of the opening. Topstitch around the edge and along the lines shown in the template, closing the opening and defining the shape of the wing. Repeat with the other wing.

15 Make a buttonhole to fit the buttons on each wing where shown on the pattern.

16 Sew the buttons onto the horse's back at the shoulder blades as seen in the photos.

Button on the wings and take to the sky.

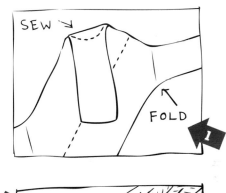

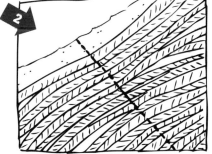

Nuts 'n Bolts Robot

See what makes this robot tick through a vinyl window on his tummy.
Hidden in his plastic bead filling are nuts and bolts . . . and elephants,
sequins, and building blocks! Find toys and bobbles to hide inside
your robot, and then spend hours trying to find them again.
You'll be amazed at how challenging it can be!

SPECIAL SKILLS »» Buttons, Beads, and Buttonholes (page 22) »» Embroidery Details (page 20)

⚡ TOOLS & MATERIALS

Basic Sewing Tool Kit (page 10)
Nuts 'n Bolts Robot template (page 131)
15 x 8-inch (38.1 x 20.3 cm) piece of fabric
2½ x 3-inch (6.4 x 7.6 cm) piece of clear vinyl
Thread to match fabric
Stuffing
Masking tape (optional)
Tissue paper

Plastic pellets (see page 14)
Funnel and spoon (for adding the
    weighted filling)
Various small objects and trinkets (plastic toys
    such as animals or cars; building blocks;
    nuts, bolts, and gears; buttons; etc.)
Embroidery floss for the mouth
2 medium buttons for the eyes
3 small colored beads for the robot's buttons

NOTE: You can buy clear vinyl at most fabric stores, but you may already have some!
Vinyl is often used as packaging for products we frequently buy, such as sheets and
blankets or bath items—so raid your linen closet before you go shopping.

⚡ INSTRUCTIONS

1 Copy the templates and cut them out.

2 Cut out two Bodies and eight Arms/Legs from the fabric. Cut one Window from the clear vinyl.

3 To assemble the arms and legs, sew each pair together with right sides facing, clip the corners in the seam allowance, and turn right side out. Lightly stuff the arms and legs with stuffing.

4 Cut out the window on the front of the robot's body where indicated by the black line. Cut diagonal lines as indicated at each corner, and fold the raw edges toward the wrong side along the gray lines. Iron the folds to crease them.

5 Stack the wrong side of the body on top of the vinyl window so that the folded edges are against the vinyl. (You may want to tape one side of the vinyl to the fabric with masking tape so that it doesn't slide; however, remove the tape before sewing over that side because the tape will gum up your needle.) Put a piece of tissue paper under your fabric and vinyl and, from the right side of the fabric, topstitch around the window. Sew around the square twice, first close to the folded edge, then ⅛ inch (3 mm) outside of the first square. This will ensure that the seam is secure, and the hidden toys and objects won't fall out of the window!

6 Pin the bodies together, right sides facing, with the arms and legs pinned into the seams and sandwiched between the body pieces. Sew around the body, leaving a 1½-inch (3.8 cm) opening in the top of the head.

7 Turn the body right side out and fill it halfway with plastic pellets using a funnel and spoon. Add a handful of various small toys. Try to be creative about what you put inside! Sew the opening closed using a ladder stitch, then sew over it a second time to make sure it's secure.

8 Embroider the mouth with floss using a backstitch. Sew on the button eyes. Securely attach a few small beads above the window for the robot's buttons.

Shake him up to scatter the toys. Then move him around with your fingers while looking through the window to find them all again. Good luck!

• •

SHOW & TELL

We all need a little attention now and then, and these projects are all about display and performance. The Knotty Frog will sit on your desk holding pencils with his elastic tongue, and you can strum the elastic strings of your Plucky Ukulele. Grabby Crab will hold notes or artwork with quilting clips sewn into his claws. Use more of your quilting clips to make a flock of Perching Birds to alight in surprising places. The Bright Ideas Computer is a fun way to store and display drawings, photographs, and notes using bias tape to create the window and lots of buttons for pretend typing. Dangle a couple of beads from your Good Times Watch to make the watch hands move with a flick of your wrist. Use a yarn needle to gauge your friends' honesty with the Lie Detector.

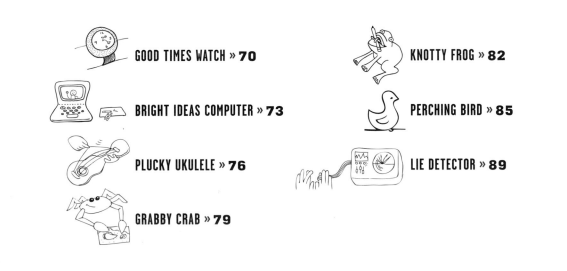

Good Times Watch

If you're stuck watching the clock, you might as well look at something fun! This brightly colored watch has beaded hands and snaps around your wrist. Bring on the good times with a flick of your wrist.

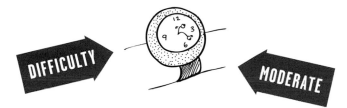

DIFFICULTY → ← MODERATE

⚡ TOOLS & MATERIALS

Basic Sewing Tool Kit (page 10)

Good Times Watch template (page 132)

10 x 5-inch (25.4 x 12.7 cm) piece of fabric for the watch body

Scrap of felt for the watch face

3 x 12-inch (7.6 x 30.5 cm) (or less) piece of fabric for the strap

Threads to match the fabrics and for topstitching

Stuffing

Small piece of hook-and-loop tape

Embroidery floss in colors of your choice

2 seed beads

Fabric glue

⚡ INSTRUCTIONS

1 Copy the templates and cut them out.

2 Cut out two watch Bodies from fabric and one watch Face from the felt. For the strap, cut two strips of fabric 1½ inches (3.8 cm) wide by the circumference of your arm plus 2 inches (5.1 cm). (My strap was about 7 inches [17.8 cm] long. The strap may be smaller for a child or bigger for an adult.)

3 Sew the two straps together with right sides facing, leaving a 2-inch (5.1 cm) opening on the side. Trim the corners and turn the strap right side out. Iron it flat, tuck the opening under, and topstitch all the way around, closing the opening.

4 Center the strap on top of one watch body, and stitch a square on the strap to secure it to the watch (**figure 1**).

5 Pin the felt face onto the front of the other watch body, and topstitch around the edge.

10 To make the hands, use all six piles of embroidery floss. Make a small stitch in the center of the watch face (indicated by the black dot on the template) and tie a double knot, leaving two long tails. Thread a small seed bead onto each tail, and tie a knot to secure the bead so it falls at the edge of the watch face. Trim the rest of the floss and add a dab of fabric glue to keep the knot secure **(figure 3)**.

It's party time!

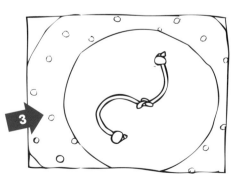

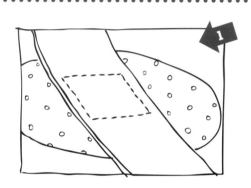

6 Fold the ends of the strap in and pin it to the center of the watch body **(figure 2)** to keep the straps out of the way while you sew the body together. Stack the other watch body on top with right sides facing so that the watch face and the strap are on the inside. Sew the watch bodies together, leaving an opening to turn. Very carefully clip slits in the seam allowance, and turn it right side out.

7 Stuff the body firmly and close the opening with a ladder stitch.

8 Cut a small square of hook-and-loop tape. Topstitch the hook tape to the top of one end of the strap and the loop tape to the underside of the other end of the strap.

9 Draw the numbers 12, 3, 6, and 9 around the face of the clock (or all the numbers if you prefer). Embroider them using a backstitch.

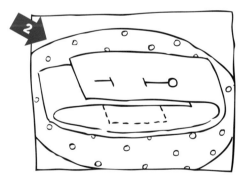

Bright Ideas Computer

This little laptop is fully equipped with brightly colored buttons, a gingham screen saver, and a data storage pocket for holding your stuff. It's just the right size for sliding a half sheet of paper into your "screen," so you can display notes, drawings, or even a 5 x 8-inch photo.

SPECIAL SKILLS » Appliqué (page 20) » Double-Fold Bias Tape (page 19)
Buttons, Beads, and Buttonholes (page 22)

✎ TOOLS & MATERIALS

Basic Sewing Tool Kit (page 10)

Bright Ideas Computer template (page 132)

4 x 6-inch (10.2 x 15.2 cm) piece of orange felt

3 x 3-inch (7.6 x 7.6 cm) piece of yellow felt

Three 10 x 13 ½-inch (25.4 x 34.3 cm) pieces of blue fabric

10 x 13 ½-inch (25.4 x 34.3 cm) piece of gingham fabric for the screen

Two 10 x 13 ½-inch (25.4 x 34.3 cm) pieces of fusible interfacing

Two 10 x 13 ½-inch (25.4 x 34.3 cm) pieces of batting

Thread to match the fabrics and for topstitching

24-inch (61 cm) length of double-fold bias tape

12 to 15 buttons in assorted sizes and colors

✎ INSTRUCTIONS

1 Enlarge the templates and cut them out.

2 Cut out the Sun Center and the Rays and Touch-Pad appliqués from the orange and yellow felt.

3 Select one blue rectangle to be the back of the computer and one to be the front. Set aside the third blue rectangle. Following the manufacturer's instructions, fuse the interfacing to the wrong side of the back and front rectangles.

« make the back »

4 Appliqué the sun on the back of the computer: first stack the circular center on top of the rays and pin it to the center of the top half as shown **(figure 1)**. Topstitch the sun to the computer around the edge of the circle.

5 Stack one piece of batting, the back of the computer facing up, and the gingham fabric facing down. Sew around all four sides, leaving a 2-inch (5.1 cm) opening in the bottom. Clip the corners of the seam allowance off and turn right side out. Iron flat, making sure all the corners point out neatly using a chopstick or other turning tool if necessary. Sew the opening closed by hand using a ladder stitch.

« make the front »

6 Topstitch the touch-pad appliqué onto the front of the computer as shown in **figure 2**.

7 Stack the other piece of batting, the front of the computer facing up, and the third blue rectangle facing down. Sew around all four sides, leaving a 2-inch (5.1 cm) opening in the bottom. Clip the corners of the seam allowance and turn right side out. Poke out the corners with a chopstick and iron the whole piece flat. Sew the opening closed by hand using a ladder stitch.

8 Center the Window template on the top half of the front of the computer and trace it with a quilting pen or chalk pencil. Cut it out along the line.

9 Now it's time to finish the raw edge of the window opening with double-fold bias tape. Open the bias tape and line up the narrow side of the tape with the raw edge of the blue fabric on the front of the computer (the side with the touch pad) with right sides facing. Fold in the end of the tape where you will begin sewing. Sew along the fold all the way around, bending carefully around the curved corners and overlapping the ends. Fold the bias tape to the back side and tuck in the fold, encasing the raw edge of the fabric inside the tape. Iron the tape flat to help the curved corners lie neatly (they will have some creases). Turn back to the front side and carefully topstitch along the folded edge of the tape, securing the back of the binding.

10 Draw three parallel lines with a quilting pen or chalk pencil on the lower half of the front of the computer above the touch pad. Arrange the buttons on these lines. I put four large buttons on the top row, five medium to large buttons on the middle row,

and four small buttons on the bottom row. Play with the arrangement so that the sizes and colors feel balanced. Once you have positioned them the way you like, mark where each one is placed, then remove them from the fabric. Sew the buttons on one at a time.

« assemble the toy »

11 Fold the computer front in half crosswise to find the center. Draw a horizontal line across the center with your quilting pen or chalk pencil as seen in **figures 1 and 2**.

12 Neatly place the computer front on top of the computer back and pin the layers together at the corners. Make sure the buttons and touch pad on the front are facing out. You should see the gingham from the inside of the computer back through the window on the computer front. Sew two lines across the center, one ¼ inch (6 mm) above the line and the other ¼ inch (6 mm) below the line. This creates a wide hinge, allowing your laptop to close neatly.

13 Starting at the top right corner, sew across the top. Then turn and sew down the long side, turning again to sew across the bottom. Backstitch on the ends. Now the front and back layers should be securely attached, and two pockets created by the openings on the side.

Time to get to work on all those bright ideas!

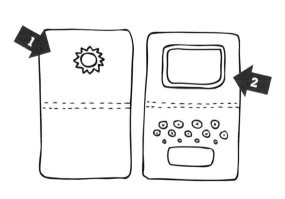

Plucky Ukulele

This ukulele is plushy and plucky! The strings are made from elastic cord and are oh-so-fun to pluck. Whether you're going to a hukilau or a sleepover, everybody loves a ukulele.

SPECIAL SKILLS »» Appliqué (page 20) »» Buttons, Beads, and Buttonholes (page 22)

⚡ TOOLS & MATERIALS

Basic Sewing Tool Kit (page 10)

Plucky Ukulele template (page 132)

10 x 13-inch (25.4 x 33 cm) piece of fusible interfacing

10 x 13-inch (25.4 x 33 cm) and 1 ½ x 37-inch (3.8 x 94 cm) pieces of heavyweight fabric*

2 x 4-inch (5.1 x 10.2 cm) piece of black felt

2 x 2-inch (5.1 x 5.1 cm) piece of white felt

Threads to match the fabric and for topstitching

4 small buttons

Stuffing

1 yard (91 cm) of elastic cord

Fabric glue

* Two shorter strips can be sewn together to make one 37-inch (94 cm) strip.

⚡ INSTRUCTIONS

1 Copy the templates and cut them out.

2 Before cutting out your shapes, iron fusible interfacing to the wrong side of the 10 x 13-inch (25.4 x 33 cm) piece of heavyweight fabric.

TIP: The form of the ukulele can easily be pulled and stretched out of shape when sewing the side on a woven fabric. Interfacing helps stabilize the fabric so that the shape of the ukulele doesn't get distorted.

3 Cut out two ukulele Bodies from the 10 x 13-inch (25.4 x 33 cm) rectangle of heavyweight fabric. From the felt, cut two Black Rectangles, one Black Circle, and one larger White Circle.

4 Appliqué the rectangles and circles onto the front of the ukulele where indicated on the template. Sew the buttons on top of the black rectangles where indicated by circles on the template.

5 Fold the end of the long strip of fabric under about 1 inch (2.5 cm) from the end and iron it flat. Starting at the fold, sew the long strip around the perimeter of the front of the ukulele, following the curves carefully. Leave 1 inch (2.5 cm) at the end of the strip. Sew the opposite side of the long strip to the back of the ukulele. Be sure to sew the strip on the back in the same direction that you sewed it on the front so that it doesn't pull unevenly. The ends should overlap in the seam allowance **(figure 1)**.

6 Clip slits carefully in the seam allowance, especially around the curves. Turn the ukulele right side out through the opening in the side and stuff it firmly. Sew the opening closed with a ladder stitch.

7 Loop the elastic cord around the bottom and top left buttons and tie a knot. Do not tie it so tight that the neck bends, but the cord should not be so loose that it sags. Trim the ends and apply a bit of fabric glue to secure the knot. Rotate the elastic so that the knot is hidden behind a button. Repeat on the remaining pair of buttons.

Aloha!

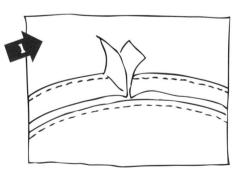

Grabby Crab

Did you know that crabs use their claws to fight, gather food, and communicate? These cute little crabs have quilting clips sewn into their claws so they can hold notes and hang from curtains. They're ready to lend a hand.

SPECIAL SKILLS »» Buttons, Beads, and Buttonholes (page 22)

TOOLS & MATERIALS

Basic Sewing Tool Kit (page 10)

Grabby Crab template (page 133)

10 x 7-inch (25.4 x 17.8 cm) piece of fabric for the body

10 x 12-inch (25.4 x 30.5 cm) piece of fabric for the legs

5 x 6-inch (12.7 x 15.2 cm) piece of felt

Thread to match the fabrics and for topstitching

2 quilting clips

Stuffing

2 medium or large shank buttons

INSTRUCTIONS

1 Copy the templates and cut them out.

2 Cut out two Bodies, four Front Legs, and eight Back Legs from the appropriate fabrics. Cut four Claws and four Claw Gussets from the felt.

3 Assemble the claws by hand. The stitches will show, so be sure to sew neatly! First sew a pair of claw gussets together along the flat edge **(figure 1a)**. Then sew each gusset to one claw piece **(figure 1b)**. Finally, lay the claw flat and sew the top and bottom pieces together along the sides, leaving it open at the base **(figure 1c)**. Repeat with the second claw.

4 Open a quilting clip and insert it into the claw. Tack the clip to the claw by stitching through the felt and around the clip several times. Repeat with the second claw, and set both aside.

5 Assemble the two front legs and four back legs by machine-sewing each pair together with right sides facing, leaving the straight ends open (leave the front legs open on both ends). Clip the corners in the seam allowance and turn them right side out. Stuff the back legs only.

6 Stack the top and bottom body pieces together with right sides facing and pin the legs in place in the seam, referring to the photo for placement. Sew the body together, securing the legs and leaving an opening in between the back legs.

7 Clip slits in the seam allowance and turn the body right side out. Stuff the body firmly and sew the opening closed with a ladder stitch.

8 Stuff the front legs from the open end. Insert the open ends into the claws and hand-stitch the claws onto the legs. Stitch over this seam twice to make sure it is secure.

9 Topstitch the legs along the joints indicated by the gray lines on the template over the stuffing. This will allow the legs to bend.

10 Stitch the shank buttons to the body. Note that the bigger the shank, the more googly the eyes will be.

What can your crab grab?

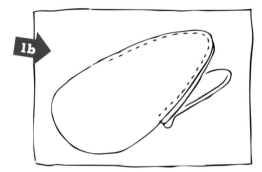

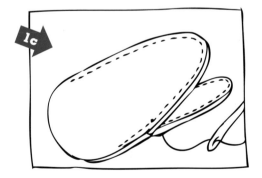

Knotty Frog

Did you know that a group of frogs is called a knot? This little frog is all alone, but he can still tie a knot! His elastic tongue can stretch and grab more than just flies. Tie a knot to keep pens, keys, and other knickknacks from flying away.

DIFFICULTY ▸ MODERATE

SPECIAL SKILLS »» Appliqué (page 20) »» Buttons, Beads, and Buttonholes (page 22)

✒ TOOLS & MATERIALS

Basic Sewing Tool Kit (page 10)

Knotty Frog template (page 133)

12 x 9-inch (30.5 x 22.9 cm) piece of green fabric

9 x 9-inch (22.9 x 22.9 cm) piece of white fabric

4 x 4-inch (10.2 x 10.2 cm) piece of pink fabric

Scraps of felt in white and green

Red hair elastic or 5 inches (12.7 cm) of pink elastic (see note)

Tissue paper

Thread to match the fabrics and for topstitching

Fabric glue

Weighted filling (page 14)

Funnel and spoon (for adding the weighted filling)

Stuffing

2 small black buttons

NOTE: I used a thick, red hair elastic for the frog's tongue. The regular skinny hair elastics are too small. An elastic hairband would also work well. Of course, you can also use 5 inches (12.7 cm) of sewing elastic if you can find it in pink or red. It may be hard to find locally, but it can be found online by searching for ballet elastic or elastic trim (just don't get the kind with lace). You can also use foldover elastic if you don't mind the indention down the middle. Look for something around ¼ inch (6 mm) wide, no bigger than ½ inch (1.3 cm).

✒ INSTRUCTIONS

1 Copy the templates and cut them out.

2 Cut out two Frog Tops from the green fabric, one Frog Bottom from the white fabric, and two pink Mouths. Cut two Eyes from the white felt and two Eyelids from the green felt.

3 To make the tongue, cut the elastic hair loop so that it is one long elastic. If there is a metal clamp, cut next to the clamp; the metal will be the wrong end hidden in the seam allowance. We will finish the raw edge on the other end to make the tongue. Set your machine to a stitch length of 0 and a moderate zigzag width. Put the raw end of your hair elastic on a piece of tissue paper and place it under your presser foot. Zigzag over the end about 10 to 20 times. The thread should now cover the raw end. Tear off the tissue paper, and dab fabric glue on the stitching to secure the thread **(figure 1)**.

4 Pin the mouths together along the flat edge, right sides facing, with the wrong end of the elastic tongue inserted in the seam allowance. Sew the pieces together along the flat edge, backstitching several times over the tongue.

5 Sew the body tops together along the curved edge of the back.

6 Turn the frog top to the right side. Center the top of the mouth on the frog top, and pin it in place. Sew the top of the mouth to the top of the frog around the curved edge.

7 Pin the frog bottom to the rest of the body and to the bottom of the mouth, lining up the edges carefully. Sew around the body and the mouth where indicated by the gray line on the template. Leave a 2-inch (5.1 cm) opening for turning.

8 Clip slits in the seam allowance. Pay special attention to the corners and curves around the legs. Be sure to cut all the way into the corners without cutting through the seam. Turn the frog right side out.

9 Topstitch two short lines on each foot to create webbed feet **(figure 2)**.

10 Fill the legs and most of the body with weighted filling. Add stuffing to fill out the shape of the head. Close the opening in the mouth with a ladder stitch.

11 Place the white eyes on the body. Make sure they're placed evenly and pin them in place. Appliqué each one by hand using a whipstitch. Center the buttons over the white circles and sew them securely to the eyes. Overlap the green eyelids on the buttons and pin them in place. Make sure they are angled symmetrically. Appliqué each one to the body using a whipstitch around the curved edge.

12 Make sure there is stuffing in the bottom lip. Then use a running stitch to anchor the mouth seam to the bottom lip **(figure 3)**.

Get tongue-tied!

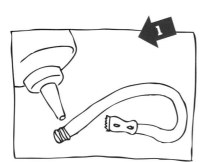
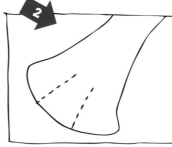

Perching Bird

These little birds are sitting pretty. With quilting clips sewn into their feet, they can perch on almost anything. Put one on your shoulder or headband, or make a flock for your clothesline. Now you have the perfect accessory for those "bird's-nest" hair days!

DIFFICULTY —————————— MODERATE

SPECIAL SKILLS »» Appliqué (page 20) »» Embroidery Details (page 20)

⚡ TOOLS & MATERIALS

Basic Sewing Tool Kit (page 10)
Perching Bird template (page 134)
8 x 10-inch (20.3 x 25.4 cm) piece of blue fabric
7 x 3-inch (17.8 x 7.6 cm) piece of orange fabric
Scrap of black felt

3 x 5-inch (7.6 x 12.7 cm) piece of black felt
Thread to match the fabrics
Stuffing
2 quilting clips
Black embroidery floss for the eyes

⚡ INSTRUCTIONS

1 Copy the templates and cut them out.

2 Cut out two Bodies and four Wings from blue fabric (one Body and two Wings in reverse), and one Tummy Gusset from the orange fabric. Cut one Beak from the black felt. Cut two full-size Feet and two Foot Gussets from the black felt.

3 Starting at the tip of the tail and with right sides together, sew the tummy gusset to one side of the body. Sew the opposite side to the other body piece with right sides together.

4 Flatten the bird so that the gusset is folded between the body pieces, and sew around the rest of the body, leaving a 1½-inch (3.8 cm) opening in the back.

5 Clip slits in the seam allowance. Turn the bird right side out and stuff the body firmly with stuffing. Sew the opening closed using a ladder stitch.

6 Fold the beak in half along the diagonal and center it on the face. Sew the beak by hand to the face along the fold using a backstitch. Secure the ends of the thread with knots hidden behind the felt.

7 Sew each pair of wings together with right sides facing, leaving a 1½-inch (3.8 cm) opening in each. Clip slits in the seam allowance, paying special attention to the corner. Turn the wings right side out and iron flat, tucking in the raw edges of the opening. Sew the openings closed using a ladder stitch.

8 Pin the wings evenly on either side of the bird. Appliqué the front edge of each wing to the body using a whipstitch. Make sure these are even and secure.

9 Assemble the feet by hand. Your stitches will show, so be sure to sew neatly! First sew the pair of foot gussets together along the straight bottom edge **(figure 1a)**. Then sew each gusset to one foot piece **(figure 1b)**. Lay it flat and sew the top and bottom pieces together along the sides **(figure 1c)**. Open a quilting clip and insert it into the foot **(figure 1d)**. Close the clip and finish sewing the foot closed **(figure 1e)**.

10 Attach the feet to the body with the curve of the quilting clip following the curve of the body. Stitch around the back of the clip several times, and make several side-to-side stitches around the clip. This will secure the clip in place while attaching it to the body.

11 Embroider the eyes with black embroidery floss using a backstitch.

Now let your bird find a new perch!

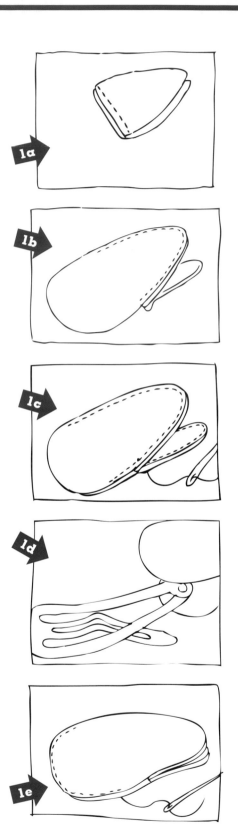

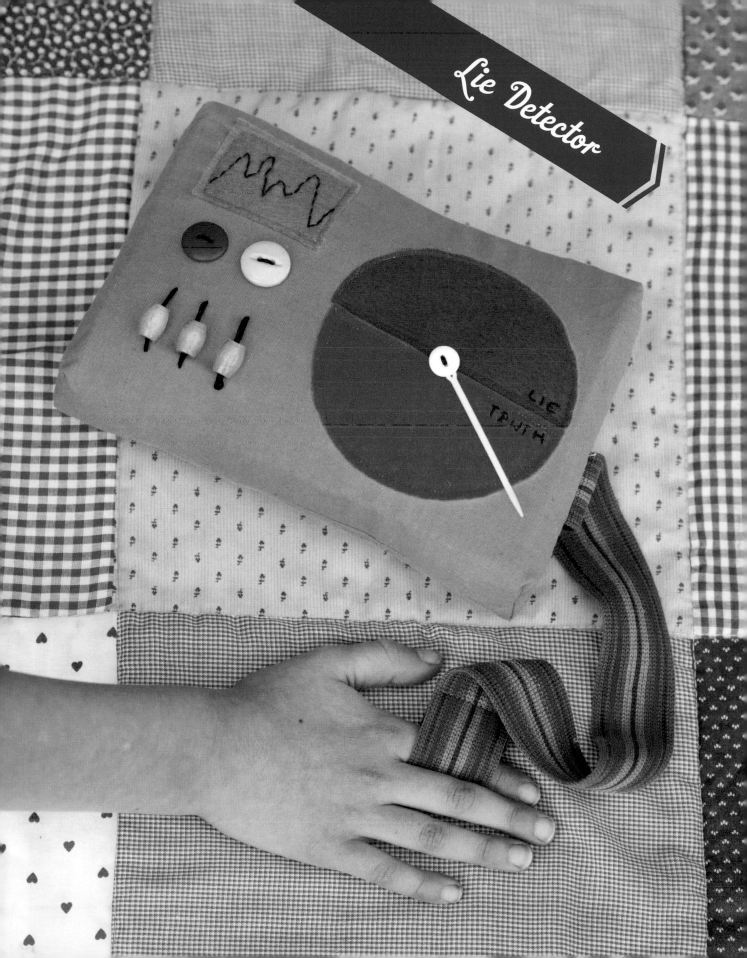

LIE

TRUTH

Lie Detector

Put your friends to the test with this retro-style lie detector. Have them slip on the finger cuff, adjust the buttons and knobs, and do your worst! When they answer a question, flick the needle and watch it spin to reveal whether they're telling a truth or a lie.

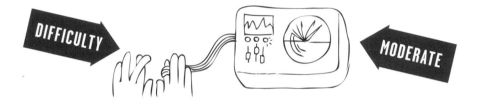

DIFFICULTY

MODERATE

SPECIAL SKILLS »» Appliqué (page 20) »» Embroidery Details (page 20)
Buttons, Beads, and Buttonholes (page 22)

✒ TOOLS & MATERIALS

Basic Sewing Tool Kit (page 10)

Lie Detector template (page 134)

15 x 10-inch (38.1 x 25.4 cm) piece of green fabric

8 x 10-inch (20.3 x 25.4 cm) sheet of plastic canvas

Scraps of felt in orange, yellow, and green

Threads to match the fabric and for topstitching

Black embroidery floss

12-inch (30.5 cm) length of ribbon, 1 inch (2.5 cm) wide, for the cuff

1 plastic yarn needle

2 small matching buttons

2 large buttons

3 medium beads

Stuffing

✒ INSTRUCTIONS

1 Copy the templates and cut them out.

2 Cut out two Bodies from the green fabric and two Plastic Canvas rectangles. Cut one orange-felt half circle and one yellow-felt half circle for the Gauge, and a green Felt Screen for the appliqués.

3 Pin the appliqués to the face of the Lie Detector one at a time and topstitch them in place.

4 Embroider the zigzag on the green screen, and the words LIE and TRUTH on the gauge.

5 With right sides facing, sew the bodies together, inserting the ribbon in one of the side seams. Leave a 7-inch (17.8 cm) opening along the upper edge.

6 Make box corners by squashing the corners so that the seams are centered and touching. Sew a diagonal seam ½ inch (1.3 cm) from the corner. Repeat for each corner. Trim the excess fabric and turn the body right side out.

7 You will attach the yarn needle to the face of the gauge somewhat like a button joint: using black embroidery floss, tie a knot at the end of the floss and sew from the back of the fabric through the center of the gauge, through one hole of a button, through the needle, through a second button, and then back down through the second button again, through the needle and the first button, to the back of the fabric. Repeat. Tie off the thread on the wrong side securely, but not too tight. The right amount of tension will allow the needle to spin easily between the buttons.

8 Sew on the remaining decorative buttons and beads as shown in the photo. Attach the beads with a long stitch so they can slide up and down.

9 Slide the plastic canvas rectangles through the opening in the top, positioning one on the top and one on the bottom. Put stuffing between the plastic rectangles until it is firm. Sew the opening closed with a ladder stitch.

10 Fold under ¼ inch (6 mm) of the raw end of the ribbon. Fold the ribbon again, about 1 to 2 inches (2.5 to 5.1 cm) from the first fold, and sew the first fold to the ribbon, catching the raw end in the seam and forming a loop.

You're finished, and that's no lie!

Cat-Fish Turnover Doll

One shape, two animals! This ambiguous softie reminds me of those vague "duck or rabbit" drawings you can stare at for hours. Turn the goldfish over to find a cat. Make this project or draw your own ambiguous shape and follow the instructions below to assemble and embellish it.

DIFFICULTY EASY

- -

SPECIAL SKILLS »» Appliqué (page 20) »» Embroidery Details (page 20)

⚡ TOOLS & MATERIALS

Basic Sewing Tool Kit (page 10)
Cat-Fish template (page 135)
10 x 6-inch (25.4 x 15.2 cm) piece of brown fabric for the cat body
10 x 6-inch (25.4 x 15.2 cm) piece of gold fabric for the fish body

Thread to match the fabrics
Stuffing
Scraps of felt in orange and white
Embroidery floss in various colors for the eyes/pupils, nose, mouth, legs, tail, and fin

- -

⚡ INSTRUCTIONS

1 Copy the templates and cut them out.

2 Cut out one Cat Body from the brown fabric and one Fish Body from the gold fabric.

3 With right sides facing, sew the bodies together, leaving a 1-inch (2.5 cm) opening along the bottom of the cat.

4 Clip slits in the seam allowance and turn the cat/fish right side out through the opening. Poke the corners out carefully with a chopstick or other turning tool, and stuff the body firmly. Stitch the opening closed using a ladder stitch.

5 Cut out an orange felt Fin and a white felt Eye for the fish. Appliqué the eye using a whipstitch, and attach the fin using a tight whipstitch along the short side.

6 Use a quilting pen or chalk pencil to draw the eyes, nose, mouth, legs, and tail on the cat, and the pupil and fins on the fish. Embroider the details in contrasting colors using a satin stitch for the eyes and a backstitch for the rest.

Now will the cat ever catch the fish?

- -

4 Unfold B and D. With right sides facing, sew C and D together on the arc where the tail is missing (indicated on the template by a gray line). Be careful to not sew over B.

5 Now, stack all four together with A on top, then B, D, and C. This will make a sandwich with like fabrics touching, and the two shapes with cut-off tops sandwiched inside.

6 Sew around the perimeter of A, starting at the top right dot shown on the template. When you reach the dots near the tail, stop and pivot your fabric with the needle still in the fabric. Sew down and back up the tail until you reach the other dot, pivoting again in the same manner. Be sure to make the pivot exactly on the arc you sewed in step 4 to make a neat tail. Stop at the other dot at the top, leaving an opening to turn.

7 Clip slits in your seam allowance perpendicular to your seam, especially in the corners. Be sure not to cut into the seam! Turn the bubble right side out and check that all of your seams are secure, and that everything turns nicely. Use a chopstick or the eraser end of a pencil, if necessary, to gently push out the tail.

8 Stuff the main body. Use small bits to first stuff the tail, pushing it all the way to the end with a chopstick or other tool. Don't overstuff the tail, but make sure the bubble is stuffed firmly and all edges are pushed out nicely. Close the opening in the top by hand using a ladder stitch.

9 Embroider your chosen phrase on the face of the bubble using a backstitch. Choose a color that contrasts with your fabric. You may embroider your message freehand, or write it first with a quilting pen or chalk pencil.

Now, don't worry! Your secret's safe with me.

HERE ARE SOME FUN IDEAS FOR SECRET MESSAGES:

I like you.
The secret to life is 42.
Will you marry me?
Look under the bed.
Secret ingredient: nutmeg
Left 32—Right 47—Left 25
You're swell.

The Caterpillar and the Butterfly

This doll doesn't just flip, it goes through metamorphoses! As a smaller pattern without some of the more intricate parts of the other flip dolls, this makes a great first flip doll to sew.

DIFFICULTY — MODERATE

SPECIAL SKILLS »» Appliqué (page 20) »» Adding Trims (page 18)
Embroidery Details (page 20)

✎ TOOLS & MATERIALS

Basic Sewing Tool Kit (page 10)

The Caterpillar and the Butterfly templates (page 136)

7 x 7-inch (17.8 x 17.8 cm) piece of green fabric for the butterfly

7 x 7-inch (17.8 x 17.8 cm) piece of green-striped fabric for the caterpillar

Batting

8 x 7-inch (20.3 x 17.8 cm) piece of black felt

Scraps of felt in white and yellow

12-inch (30.5 cm) length of ball fringe

Threads to match the fabrics and for topstitching

Embroidery floss for the eyes

Two 3-inch (7.6 cm) lengths of rickrack or other ribbon trim

✎ INSTRUCTIONS

1 Copy the templates and cut them out.

2 Cut one Body Top and two Body Bottoms from both the green fabric and the green-striped fabric. Cut two Body Top pieces from the batting, and then cut one of them in half lengthwise to make the bottom pieces. Cut two black felt Wings and cut out the smaller wing details from white and yellow felt. Cut two pieces of ball fringe 4 inches (10.1 cm) long.

« make the butterfly »

3 Appliqué the white and yellow details onto the wings with matching thread, as shown on the template, using a whipstitch. Set aside.

4 To make the bottom of the body, stack the two bottom halves with right sides facing and place one of the bottom batting pieces on top. Line up the batting with the outside edge (the curved edges). Sew 1 inch (2.5 cm) at the bottom and 1 inch (2.5 cm) at the top of the straight inside edge of the batting, leaving it open in the middle (**figure 1**). Open the bottom and iron, pressing the seams open.

5 Stack the body top on the bottom with right sides facing, then put the other layer of batting on top. Sew all the way around the body. Clip slits in the seam allowance, then turn right side out.

6 Pin the wings on top of the body, then sew them to the body along the gray line shown in the template. You may sew them by hand or topstitch the wings using your sewing machine. If you sew them by machine, carefully separate the bottom opening so that you don't stitch through the bottom layer.

« make the caterpillar »

7 Make the bottom of the caterpillar's body in the same manner as the butterfly (described in step 4).

8 Layer the top and bottom bodies with right sides facing, pinning the ball trim in between with the pompoms on the inside. Make sure the ribbon part of the trim is in the seam allowance—you want to sew over the threads connecting the pompoms to the ribbon. Sew all the way around the body with your needle in the left-hand position. This will allow you to sew close to the balls, connect the two layers, and catch the ball trim in the

seam. Make sure all seams are secure and clip notches in the seam allowance.

« combine the dolls »

9 With the caterpillar wrong side out and the butterfly right side out, carefully push the caterpillar inside the butterfly, lining up the bottom openings. Pin them together and hand-sew the openings together along the pressed seam using a ladder stitch. Go around the opening once with large stitches, then a second time with smaller stitches.

10 Embroider eyes on the caterpillar and butterfly. Stitch small rickrack or other ribbon trim onto the top of the head for antennae.

Ta da! To flip the caterpillar into a butterfly, put your index fingers inside the head and tail and then push from the outside with your thumbs. Smooth out the wings and neatly poke out the edges. You can put a finger inside the butterfly like you would a puppet if you want her to "fly!"

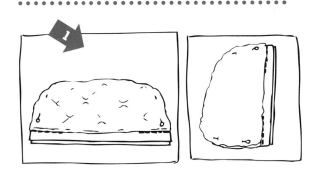

George and the Dragon

The classic story of Saint George and the Dragon combined with fun details make this my absolute favorite project. George has a little flip-up visor, an embroidered mustache, and a yarn plume. The dragon has rickrack spines, bubbly eyes, and orange toenails. Beware—all these details take some time, but the final doll is well worth it! See the notes on page 25 to make a pair of rag dolls instead of a flip doll.

DIFFICULTY —▶ ◀— ADVANCED

SPECIAL SKILLS »» Adding Trims (page 18) »» Buttons, Beads, and Buttonholes (page 22) Embroidery Details (page 20) »» Appliqué (page 20)

⚡ TOOLS & MATERIALS

Basic Sewing Tool Kit (page 10)

George and the Dragon template (page 136–137)

20 x 18-inch piece of gray fabric

8 x 12-inch piece of accent fabric

4 x 3-inch piece of flesh-colored fabric

18 x 16-inch piece of green fabric

8 x 10-inch piece of orange fabric

3 x 2-inch piece of red felt

6 x 3-inch piece of white felt

1 yard of batting

Threads to match the fabrics and for topstitching, including black

10-inch length of medium or jumbo rickrack

Stuffing

12-inch length of black ribbon or twill tape plus 12 inches (optional) for trimming the helmet

2 medium buttons

Embroidery floss for George's mustache, mouth, and nose, and for the dragon's yellow toenails

1 yard of medium-weight yarn for the plume

⚡ INSTRUCTIONS

1 Copy the templates and cut them out.

2 Cut out two Bodies, six Arms/Legs (reversing three), and two Visors from the gray fabric. Cut two Skirts from the accent fabric, and one flesh-colored Face. Cut two Dragon Bodies and two Legs in green (reversing one of each). Cut four dragon Wings in orange (reversing two), two Dragon Eyes in white felt, one small red felt Shield, and one small white felt Cross. Cut one George Body, one Visor, two Dragon Bodies, and two Wings from batting.

NOTE Keep a hot iron available to press seams as you sew. This will help make the assembly neat, and you'll be less likely to make mistakes.

« make the dragon »

3 Pin the dragon bodies, right sides facing, between the two layers of batting. Sew along the straight side of the tummy. To add a scaly texture to your dragon's body, unfold the body and lay it right side up. With a chalk pencil or quilting pen, draw scalloped scales on the body. Either by hand or by machine, stitch along these lines through the green fabric and the batting to create quilted scales (**figure 1**).

4 Pin together each pair of wings with right sides facing and a batting wing on the bottom. Sew along the curved edges, leaving the flat edge open. Clip slits in the seam allowance all the way around, being careful not to cut through the seam. Turn the wing right side out, poking out all edges neatly, and iron it flat. Repeat with the second wing.

5 Pin the open edge of each wing to the dragon's shoulders (**figure 2**). Sew the wings to the body.

6 Fold the dragon bodies with right sides facing again. Pin the bodies together, placing the rickrack in the seam from the top of the head, down along the dragon's back, and ending at the tip of the tail. Pin the center of the rickrack where the seam will be sewn so that half of the rickrack is on the outside and half is unseen inside. (To make sure your rickrack doesn't shift, you can sew it to one side before sewing all the layers together.) Sew from the nose, along the back, to the underside of the tail, securing the rickrack and sewing over the stitches that hold the wings in place. Then sew from the nose down the tummy.

7 Clip small slits in the seam allowance all the way around the body right up to the seam, paying special attention to sharp corners. Turn the dragon right side out and make sure that all the seams are sewn neatly. Correct any mistakes now! Then, poke the edges out, and iron to help the seams lie nicely.

« make george »

8 Sew each pair of arms together with right sides facing, leaving the end open. Clip slits in the seam allowance and turn right side out. Stuff firmly and set aside. Repeat this process with the legs; however, sew each gray leg to one of the dragon's green legs.

9 Trace the shape of the face onto George's head with a quilting pen or chalk pencil. Draw a second oval within the first about

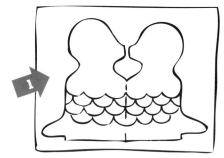
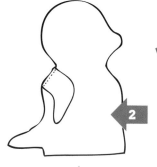
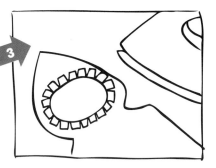

¼ inch (6 mm) smaller than the original. Neatly cut out the smaller oval, and then cut small perpendicular slits in the ¼ inch all the way around.

10 With the body lying face down, fold the ¼-inch tabs back to the wrong side and iron flat (figure 3). It may help to use a ruler or pencil to hold the edges down as you move the iron so that you don't burn your fingers. Pin the face to the back of the opening so that the folded tabs are between the face and the front of the body.

11 With George facing up, topstitch around the face opening close to the folded edge. If you want to dress up this edge, you can topstitch a black ribbon or twill tape around the edge of the face, turning under the end; it may be neater to sew once around the outer edge of the trim, then again around the inner edge to help it lie flat.

12 With the body still facing up, fold the bottom edge of the front body piece up where indicated by the gray line on the pattern. Sew a small upside-down V on the fold (figure 4). Clip a slit in the center of the V all the way to the point, and then turn the fold right side out. Poke out the corners neatly with a chopstick or pencil, and iron the piece flat.

13 Pin the skirt to the wrong side of the body, lining it up with the edge of the body that you folded under. Sew the skirt to the body along the waistline, catching the raw edge of the body that was folded up in the seam.

14 Fold the bottom edge of the back body piece up with right sides facing where indicated by the gray line, as you did for the front. Iron it flat and pin the second skirt piece to the wrong side of the body piece as before. Sew across the long horizontal edge, catching the raw edge of the body that was folded up in the seam.

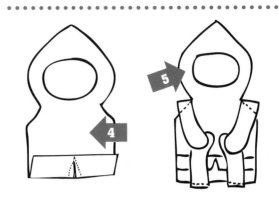

15 Cut two 6-inch (15.2 cm) lengths of black ribbon or twill tape. Topstitch them over the seams where you attached George's skirt. The black ribbon creates a belt and neatens up your seams.

16 Pin the arms to George's shoulders so that they curve inward and sew them to the body. Repeat with the legs, sewing them to the bottom edge of George's front (figure 5).

17 Pin the front and back of the body together with the arms and legs folded in and a layer of batting on the bottom. Sew around the perimeter of the body, leaving the bottom open. Leave a 2-inch (5.1 cm) opening in the side of George's body.

18 Clip small slits in the seam allowance, paying special attention to sharp corners. Turn George right side out to make sure that all the seams are neatly sewn. Correct any mistakes now. Then poke all the edges out and iron to help the seams lie neatly.

19 Pin the two visors together with right sides facing and a layer of batting on the bottom. Sew around the visor, leaving a short side open. Clip the corners in the seam allowance and turn the visor right side out. Fold in the open edges, and iron seams flat. Topstitch around the perimeter of the visor, closing the open edge.

20 On each end of the visor, sew a buttonhole to fit the buttons.

21 Stitch five lines onto the front of the visor using black thread, a short stitch length, and a wide zigzag stitch. Backstitch on each end to prevent unraveling.

22 Sew a button on either side of George's face, just inside the seam.

23 Embroider George's mustache and eyes with a satin stitch and his eyebrows and nose with a backstitch.

« create the flip »

24 Turn George wrong side out and the dragon right side out. Insert the dragon inside George. Pin the bottom edges together, centering the dragon's tummy seam in the middle of George's front. Sew the dolls together.

25 Pull the dragon out from George's body. You should now see the wrong side of both dolls, joined at the bottom. With your machine stitch length set at 0 and a wide zigzag, stitch the center tops of the heads together in the seam allowance (**figure 6**). These stitches will not show on the outside but will anchor the heads together.

26 Turn the doll right side out through the hole in George's side. Stitch the opening in the bottom seam closed with a ladder stitch.

27 Button the visor onto George's head. Appliqué the red shield and white cross to George's chest using a whipstitch.

28 To make the plume, cut the yarn into three 12-inch (30.5 cm) lengths and loosely braid them together, tying a knot at each end. Accordion-fold the braid three times. With a needle and thread, stitch the base of the plume together, going through the bottom of each fold, as shown in the diagram (**figure 7**). When the folds are secure, stitch it to the top of George's head with five or six strong stitches.

29 Flip the doll to the dragon side. Embroider three orange (or some other gruesome color) toenails on each foot.

30 Appliqué the eyes to the dragon's head using a whipstitch. Tuck a small amount of batting under each circle before finishing the stitches to give the eye some shape. Embroider his pupils with a satin stitch.

All done! Now you're ready to tell the story of George and the Dragon!

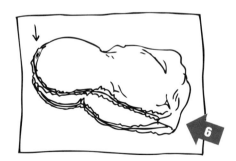

The Owl and the Pussycat

Recite "The Owl and the Pussycat" with this modern version of the traditional flip doll. Turn the owl inside out and find the kitty hiding inside. This is a fairly simple flip doll—definitely doable for a first attempt!

DIFFICULTY → ← MODERATE

- -

SPECIAL SKILLS »» Embroidery Details (page 20) »» Adding Trims (page 18) »» Appliqué (page 20)

✎ TOOLS & MATERIALS

Basic Sewing Tool Kit (page 10)

The Owl and the Pussycat template (page 138)

14 x 11-inch (35.6 x 27.9 cm) piece of brown fabric for the owl

6 x 5-inch (15.2 x 12.7 cm) piece of accent fabric for the owl

14 x 15-inch (35.6 x 38.1 cm) piece of orange fabric for the cat

Scraps of felt in white, orange, blue, brown, or other colors as desired

14 x 11-inch (35.6 x 27.9 cm) piece of low-loft batting

Threads to match the fabrics

Embroidery floss for the cat's eyes, nose, mouth, and whiskers, and the owl's pupils

6-inch (15.2 cm) length of rickrack

- -

✎ INSTRUCTIONS

1 Copy the templates and cut them out.

2 Cut out nine pattern pieces: one Owl Body, one Owl Head, and two owl Wings (one in reverse) from brown fabric; one Owl Tummy from the accent fabric; and two Cat Bodies and two cat Tails from the orange fabric. Cut the details from the felt in your choice of colors or as pictured: two big circles for the owl's Eyes, two smaller circles for the owl's Pupils, one owl Beak, and one cat Muzzle. Cut two Owl Bodies and two Cat Bodies from the low-loft batting.

« make the pussycat »

3 With right sides facing, sew the two tails together, leaving the straight end open. Clip slits around the curved end, and turn it right side out. Iron flat so that the seams lie neatly. Center the tail on the bottom of the cat's back, pin, and sew in place.

4 Lay the front body piece on top of the back body piece with right sides facing and the tail sandwiched in between. Lay one piece of batting on the bottom and one on the top. Pin all the edges together. Sew the sandwich together around the sides and top, leaving the bottom open and a 2-inch (5.1 cm) opening in the middle of one side of the body.

5 Clip small slits all the way around the body in the seam allowance right up to the seam, paying special attention to the neck. Turn the cat right side out, checking that all the seams are neatly sewn. Repair any if needed. Once finished, poke all the edges out and iron them to help the seams lie neatly.

6 Stitch the felt muzzle onto the face using a whipstitch. Before finishing all the stitches, tuck a little bit of batting under the felt. Embroider the nose and eyes with a satin stitch and the mouth with a basic backstitch where indicated on the template. Make whiskers with embroidery floss: start with a tiny stitch and tie the two ends of the floss in a knot, leaving a long tail on both sides. Repeat for each whisker, making two or three on each side as shown.

« make the owl »

7 With right sides facing, lay the owl's head over his tummy, lining up the neck's edge with the top edge of the body. Put the rickrack between the two layers of fabric and pin it in place. Sew across the neck, securing the rickrack.

8 To attach the wings, first fold the bottom and inside edges toward the back along the gray line shown in the template. Iron the folds flat, and clip the corners so that they will lie nicely. Pin them onto the body, lining up the outer edges and overlapping the neck seam. Topstitch along the folded edges to secure them.

9 Lay the front body piece on top of the back body piece with right sides facing. Then lay one piece of batting on the bottom and one on the top. Pin all the edges together. Sew the sandwich together around the sides and top, leaving the bottom open.

10 Clip small slits in the seam allowance all the way around the body right up to the seam, paying special attention to the neck. Turn the owl right side out, checking that all the seams are neatly sewn. Repair any seams if needed. Once that's finished, poke all the edges out and iron them to help the seams lie neatly.

11 Appliqué the big felt circles to the owl's face by hand using a backstitch, and then stitch the small circles onto the big circles. Embroider small pupils inside the small felt circles. Appliqué the felt beak onto the owl's face with a whipstitch.

« create the flip »

12 Turn the owl right side out and the cat wrong side out. Insert the owl inside the cat, lining up the side seams. Make sure they are face to face on the inside. Pin the bottom edges together.

13 Use a ½-inch (1.3 cm) seam allowance to sew the bottoms together.

14 Pull the cat out from the owl's body so that you see the wrong side of both animals, joined at the bottom. Fold the doll in half at the seam so that the cat is lying on top of the owl, and line up the center top of the animals' heads. With your stitch length set at 0 and a wide zigzag, stitch the center tops of the heads together in the seam allowance **(figure 1)**. These stitches will not show on the outside but they will anchor the heads together.

15 Turn the doll right side out through the hole in the cat's side. Now your two dolls are connected at the bottom, and the owl is inside of the cat. Stitch the opening closed with a ladder stitch.

Time to flip! Just turn it inside out like you would a sock—gently tugging on the ears to pull the head out.

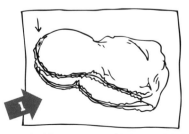

CLEARY HENRY and the Paper Ro

Superhero Flip Doll

For this doll, instead of making two characters, you're making one character in two different costumes. He or she is ready for a quick change at a moment's notice. Meet one of America's favorite transforming characters: the superhero!

SPECIAL SKILLS »» Making Hair (page 20) »» Appliqué (page 20) »» Adding Trims (page 18) Embroidery Details (page 20)

⚡ TOOLS & MATERIALS

Basic Sewing Tool Kit (page 10)

Superhero Flip Doll template (page 139)

10 x 6-inch (25.4 x 15.2 cm) piece of flesh-colored fabric

18 x 6-inch (45.7 x 15.2 cm) piece of nonfraying fabric (such as fleece) for the hair

4 x 6-inch (10.2 x 15.2 cm) piece of fabric for the superhero's pants

22 x 16-inch 55.9 x 40.6 cm) piece of fabric for the superhero's shirt, arms, and legs

10 x 6-inch (25.4 x 15.2 cm) piece of fabric for the alter ego's shirt and arms

10 x 6-inch (25.4 x 15.2 cm) piece of fabric for the alter ego's pants and legs

Scraps of felt for the mask, stars, and optional tie

½ yard (45.7 cm) of batting

Threads to match the fabrics

Lace or other trim (optional)

Stuffing

Embroidery floss for the eyes, mouths, and other details as desired (glasses, buttons, etc.)

⚡ INSTRUCTIONS

1 Copy the templates and cut them out.

> **NOTE:** You need to add a ¼-inch (6 mm) seam allowance where the body is sewn together at the neck and waist!

2 Cut the following pieces from the following fabrics:

> »» Cut out two Heads from the flesh-colored fabric and two Heads from the hair fabric, adding a ¼-inch (6 mm) seam allowance to the neck edge of each one.

> »» Cut one Boy Hair or one Girl Hair and four Pigtails (reversing two of them) from

the hair fabric (depending on whether you are making a boy or girl alter ego).

» Cut two Bottoms from the superhero's pants fabric and two Bottoms from the alter ego's pants fabric, adding a ¼-inch (6 mm) seam allowance to the top edge of each one.

» Cut two Tops from the superhero's shirt fabric and two Tops from the alter ego's shirt fabric, adding a ¼-inch (6 mm) seam allowance to both the top and the bottom edges of each one.

» Cut six Arms/Legs from the superhero's arm/leg fabric (reversing three of them).

» Cut four Arms from the alter ego's shirt fabric (reversing two) and two Legs from the alter ego's pants fabric (reversing one).

» Cut one Mask (choose which shape), one Star, and one Tie (if you're making a boy) in your choice of felt colors.

» Cut two full body pieces from the batting.

« assemble the bodies »

3 Topstitch the girl hair or boy hair to one head. Topstitch the mask to the face of the superhero.

4 Sew the superhero head to the super-hero's shirt along the neck with a ¼-inch (6 mm) seam. Sew the shirt to the superhero's pants along the waist with a ¼-inch (6 mm) seam. Now you have the front of the super-hero. Do the same with the superhero head cut from the hair fabric, shirt, and pants for the back. Repeat for the alter ego's front and back.

5 Topstitch the star to the superhero's front. Topstitch the tie (for a boy) or a lacy trim (for a girl) to the alter ego's front.

6 Next, sew each pair of arms together, two for the superhero and two for the alter ego, with right sides facing. Clip slits in the seam allowances and turn right side out. Stuff them firmly and pin to the shoulders of the front of each body. Sew them to the body.

7 The dolls will share a pair of legs. Sew each superhero leg to an alter ego leg with right sides facing. Clip slits in the seam allowances and turn them right side out. Stuff them firmly and pin them to the bottom of the superhero bodies. Make sure the fabric facing out matches the superhero's pants. Sew them to the body.

8 If you're making a girl doll, sew the two pairs of pigtails together with right sides facing. Clip slits in the seam allowances and turn them right side out. Stuff firmly and pin them to the sides of each head. Sew them to the heads.

9 Pin the front and back of each body together with the arms and legs folded in and a layer of batting on the bottom. Sew around the perimeter of each body, leaving the bottom open. Leave a 2-inch (5.1 cm) opening in the side of the alter ego's body.

10 Clip slits in the seam allowance for each doll. Pay special attention to the corner of the neck. Turn right side out and make sure all the seams are secure and the arms are sewn neatly into the seam. Correct any mistakes now!

11 Embroider eyes and a mouth on each doll's face. Add any other embroidery, like buttons or glasses, now as well.

« join the bodies »

12 Turn the alter ego inside out again. Insert the superhero, still right side out, inside the alter ego. Make sure they are facing

each other. Pin the bottom edges together, first lining up the seams.

13 Sew around the bottom edge. Be sure to sew over the stitching where you attached the legs. Go around twice to make this seam very secure.

14 Pull the superhero out of the alter ego so that you see the wrong side of both dolls, joined at the bottom. Fold the doll in half at the seam so that the superhero is lying on top of the alter ego, and line up the center top of their heads. With your machine's stitch length set at 0 and a wide zigzag, stitch the center tops of the heads together in the seam allowance **(figure 1)**. These stitches will not show on the outside but they will anchor the heads together.

15 Turn the doll right sides out through the hole in the alter ego's body. The two dolls now are connected at the bottom, and the superhero is inside of the alter ego. Stitch the opening closed with a ladder stitch.

Time to flip! Just turn it inside out like you would a sock—gently tugging on the ears to pull the head out.

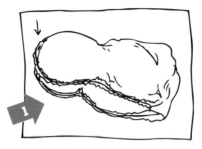

Vampire and Bat

Can vampires really turn into bats? This one does! Tell one of the countless vampire stories with this cute count. When your vampire is ready to make a quick exit, turn him into a bat and let him fly away!

DIFFICULTY

ADVANCED

SPECIAL SKILLS »» Making Hair (page 20) »» Appliqué (page 20) »» Embroidery Details (page 20)

⚡ TOOLS & MATERIALS

Basic Sewing Tool Kit (page 10)

Vampire and Bat template (page 140)

5 x 5-inch (12.7 x 12.7 cm) piece of white fabric for the vampire's face

5 x 8-inch (12.7 x 20.3 cm) piece of black fleece for the vampire's hair

10 x 10-inch (25.4 x 25.4 cm) piece of gray fabric for the vampire's body

20 x 14-inch (60.8 x 35.6 cm) piece of black knit fabric for the bat (see note)

4 x 2-inch (10.2 x 5.1 cm) piece of accent fabric for the bat's ears

Scraps of felt in yellow, black, dark gray, and white

20 x 12-inch (60.8 x 30.5 cm) piece of batting

Threads to match the fabrics and for topstitching

6-inch (15.2 cm) length of red bias tape

Stuffing

Embroidery floss for the vampire's nose, mouth, and teeth

NOTE: I used a black knit fabric for the bat's body, fleece for the vampire's hair, and quilting cottons for the vampire's body. Combining the quilting cottons with fabrics that have a little bit of stretch will make flipping the doll back and forth easier without losing the shape of the body.

✎ INSTRUCTIONS

1 Copy the templates and cut them out.

2 Cut out one Head from white fabric, adding a ¼-inch (6 mm) seam allowance at the neck. Cut one Head and one Hair in black fleece. From the gray fabric, cut two Bodies, adding a ¼-inch (6 mm) seam allowance at the neck, and four Arms/Legs (reversing two). Cut four Arms/Legs, four Wings, two Ears (reversing half of the Arms/Legs, Wings, and Ears), and two Bat Bodies from the black knit fabric. Cut two Ears (reversing one) from the accent fabric. Cut four large Eyes from yellow felt, four smaller Eyes from black felt, one Nose from dark gray felt, and one Bat Mouth from white felt. Cut one vampire (Head and Body), one Bat Body, and two Wings from the batting.

. . . .

NOTICE that you need to add a ¼-inch (6 mm) seam allowance where the body is sewn together at the neck!

. . . .

« make the vampire »

3 Topstitch the hair to the vampire's face. Topstitch the bias tape down the center of the vampire's body where indicated by the gray line on the template.

4 Sew the vampire's face to his body along the neck with a ¼-inch (6 mm) seam allowance to make the front. Do the same with the fleece head and body for the back.

5 Sew the two pairs of gray arms together with right sides facing. Clip slits in the seam allowance and turn them right side out. Stuff them firmly and pin them to the shoulders on the front of the vampire's body. Sew them to the body.

6 Sew the two pairs of black legs together with right sides facing. Clip slits in the seam allowance and turn them right side out. Stuff them firmly and pin them to the waist at the front of the vampire's body. Sew them to the body.

7 Pin the front and back of the body together with the arms and legs folded in and a layer of batting on the bottom. Sew around the perimeter of the body, leaving the bottom open. Leave a 2-inch (5.1 cm) opening in one side of the vampire's body.

8 Clip slits in the seam allowance. Turn the vampire right side out and make sure that all the seams are secure and the arms are sewn neatly into the seam. Correct any mistakes now!

9 Appliqué the large yellow eyes to the vampire's face with matching thread using a whipstitch, then appliqué the small black eyes with matching thread on top of the yellow. Embroider the nose, mouth, and teeth using a backstitch.

« make the bat »

10 Pin each pair of bat wings together with right sides facing and a layer of batting on the bottom. Sew them together, leaving the side of the wing marked with a gray line on the template open. Clip slits in the seam allowance and turn them right side out.

11 Pin the wings to either side of the front of the bat body. Sew them to the body.

12 Sew each pair of ears together with right sides facing. Clip slits in the seam allowance and turn them right side out. Pin them to the front of the bat body with the accent fabric facing against the bat. Sew them to the bat.

13 Pin the front and back of the bat body together with the wings folded in and a layer of batting on the bottom. Sew around the perimeter of the body, leaving the bottom open.

14 Clip slits in the seam allowance. Turn the bat right side out and make sure that all the seams are secure and the wings and ears are sewn neatly into the seam. Correct any mistakes now!

15 Appliqué the large yellow eyes to the bat's face using a whipstitch, then appliqué the small black eyes on top of the yellow. Appliqué the nose and mouth also.

« join the bodies »

16 Turn the vampire inside out again. Insert the bat, still right side out, inside the vampire. Make sure they are facing each other, and line up the seams. Pin the bottom edges together.

17 Sew around the bottom edge. Be sure to sew over the stitching where you attached the legs. Go around twice to make this seam secure.

18 Pull the bat out of the vampire so that you see the wrong side of both dolls, joined at the bottom. Fold the doll in half at the seam so that the bat is lying on top of the vampire, and line up the center top of their heads. With your stitch length set at 0 and a wide zigzag, stitch the center tops of the heads together in the seam allowance (**figure 1**). These stitches will not show on the outside but they will anchor the heads together.

19 Turn the doll right sides out through the hole in the vampire's body. The two dolls now are connected at the bottom, and the bat is inside of the vampire. Stitch the opening closed with a ladder stitch.

Time to flip! Just turn it inside out like you would a sock—gently tugging on the ears to pull the head out.

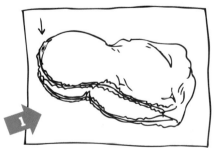

Circus Flip Doll

This doll brings together the traditional topsy-turvy skirted doll with a few nontraditional characters. Meet the bearded lady and the conjoined twins!

SPECIAL SKILLS »» Making Hair (20) »» Adding Trims (page 18) »» Appliqué (page 20)
Embroidery Details (page 20)

✎ TOOLS & MATERIALS

Basic Sewing Tool Kit (page 10)

Circus Flip Doll template (page 141)

10 x 6-inch (25.4 x 15.2 cm) piece of flesh-colored fabric for the conjoined twins

4½ x 4½-inch (11.4 x 11.4 cm) piece of flesh-colored fabric for the bearded lady

20 x 13-inch (50.8 x 33 cm) piece of gingham fabric

17 x 13-inch (43.2 x 33 cm) piece of red fabric

9 x 5-inch (22.9 x 12.7 cm) piece of black fleece

4 x 3-inch (10.2 x 7.6 cm) piece of black felt

2 x 1-inch (5.1 x 2.5 cm) piece of white felt

Threads to match the fabrics and for topstitching

Stuffing

18-inch (45.7 cm) length of trim for each skirt (36 inches [91 cm] total)

6 skeins of yellow embroidery floss for the twins' hair

Tissue paper

Ribbon, yarn, or embroidery floss for the twins' hair bows

Embroidery floss for eyes, lips/mouths, and buttons

✎ INSTRUCTIONS

1 Copy the templates and cut them out.

2 Cut out two Conjoined Twins bodies and one Bearded Lady Head from the appropriate pieces of flesh-colored fabric. Cut two Conjoined Twins Dresses, four Arms (reversing two), and two 8½ x 8½-inch (21.6 x 21.6 cm) squares (for their skirt) from the gingham fabric. Cut two Bearded Lady Dresses, four Arms (reversing two), and two 8½ x 8½-inch (21.6 x 21.6 cm) squares (for her skirt) from the red fabric. Cut one Bearded Lady Head and one Bearded Lady Bangs from the black fleece. Cut one Beard and Mustache from the black felt. Cut two Collars from the white felt.

« make the bearded lady »

3 Topstitch the bearded lady's bangs to her head.

4 Sew the bearded lady's face to her dress along the neck. Do the same with the bearded lady's fleece head and the other dress to make her back.

5 Sew the two pairs of red arms together with right sides facing. Clip slits in the seam allowance and turn them right side out. Stuff them firmly and pin them to the front shoulders of the bearded lady's body. Sew them to the body.

6 Pin the bodies together, right sides facing, with the arms folded in. Sew the front and back together, leaving the waist (the straight, lower edge) open and a 1½-inch (3.8 cm) opening in the top of the head.

7 Clip slits in the seam allowance. Pay special attention to the corner of the neck. Turn right side out and make sure that all the seams are secure and the arms are sewn neatly into the seam. Correct any mistakes now!

« make the conjoined twins »

8 To make the conjoined twins' dress and body, fold the neck of each dress along the gray lines shown on the template and iron the folds. Topstitch the dresses to the front and back of the body along the neck.

9 Sew the two pairs of pink arms together with right sides facing. Clip slits in the seam allowance and turn right side out. Stuff them firmly and pin them to the front shoulders of the conjoined twins' body. Sew them to the body.

10 Pin the bodies together with right sides facing, with the arms folded in. Sew the front and back together, leaving the waist (the straight, lower edge) open.

11 Clip slits in the seam allowance. Pay special attention to the V shape between the twins' two heads. Turn right side out and make sure that all the seams are secure and the arms are sewn neatly into the seam. Correct any mistakes now!

join the bodies »

12 Turn the bearded lady wrong side out. Insert the conjoined twins inside the body of the bearded lady and line up their waists, matching the seams. Pin the waists together and sew all the way around.

13 Turn the dolls right side out through the hole in the bearded lady's head. Stuff them firmly and sew the opening in the head closed with a ladder stitch.

« finish the doll »

14 Make the skirts as shown in figure 1. First sew each pair of rectangles together along one side (**figure 1a**). Then sew the two pairs together along one long side (**figure 1b**). This seam will be the hemline. Add trims to each skirt 1 inch (2.5 cm) from the hemline (**figure 1c**). Make a basting stitch around the waistline on both ends of the skirt, then pull the thread ends to gather the two waists to about 6½ inches (16.5 cm) (**figure 1d**). Sew the other side of the skirts together, creating a tube (**figure 1e**). Fold one skirt inside the other along the hem so that the wrong sides are facing (**figure 1f**).

15 Slip the skirt onto your dolls, matching the fabrics to the bodies. Hand-stitch the bearded lady's gathered waistline to her waist. Turn the raw edges under as you stitch around the first time, then stitch around the waist a second time to make it secure. Flip the skirt, revealing the conjoined twins, and attach their skirt in the same manner.

16 Appliqué the beard to the bearded lady's face with matching thread using a whipstitch along the top edge only. Appliqué the mustache to the face, slightly overlapping the beard. Appliqué the collars to the conjoined twins' dress along their necklines with matching thread using a whipstitch.

17 Make the twins' wigs using embroidery floss. For the first wig, cut three skeins

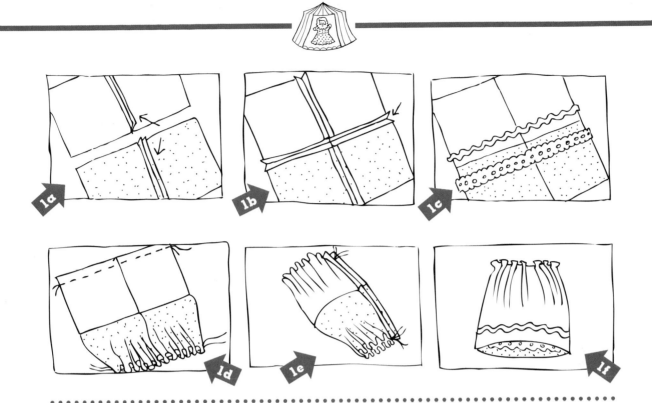

in half along one of the folds. Flatten the floss on the tissue paper, spreading it out about 1½ inches (3.8 cm) wide. Sew a line down the center of the floss on the sewing machine two or three times **(figure 2)**. Tear the tissue paper away from the seam. Place the wig on one twin's head and hand-stitch through the wig and the head with matching thread along the seam to secure it. Repeat for the second wig and twin. Give one twin braids and the other pigtails so you can tell them apart. Tie ribbons in their hair.

18 Embroider eyes and lips on the bearded lady—and be sure to give her eyelashes! Embroider the faces and buttons on the conjoined twins.

Now they're all dolled up for the circus. Come see the show!

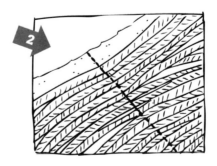

TEMPLATES

Templates in this book include a ¼-inch (6 mm) seam allowance unless otherwise stated. All templates except the Smiling Crocodile are printed at 50%. That means you will need to enlarge them on a copier 200%.

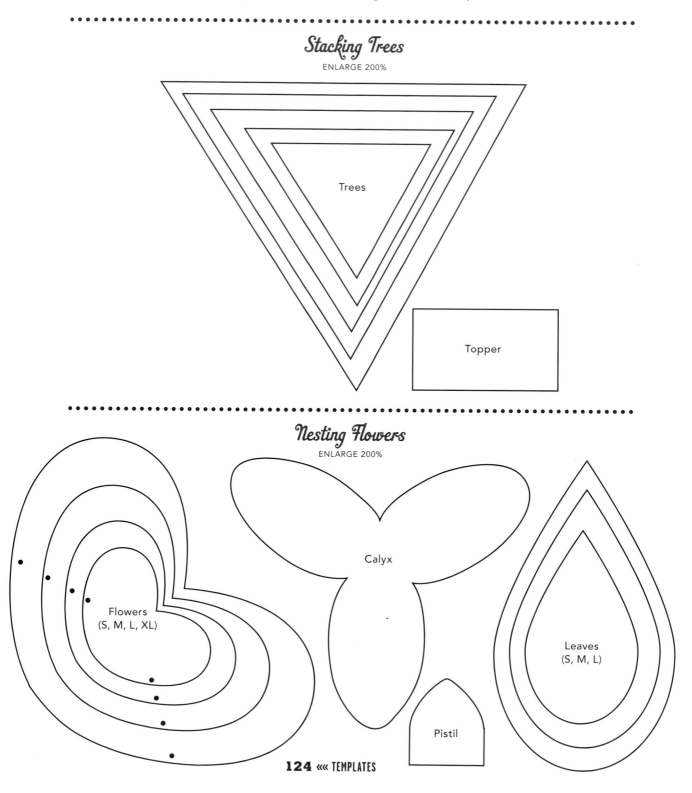

Stacking Trees

ENLARGE 200%

Trees

Topper

Nesting Flowers

ENLARGE 200%

Flowers
(S, M, L, XL)

Calyx

Leaves
(S, M, L)

Pistil

Elephant Parade

ENLARGE 200%

Ear

Body

Cheshire Cat

ENLARGE 200%

Gusset

Body

Pocket

Mouths

Tail

Smiling Crocodile

THIS TEMPLATE IS SHOWN AT 100% FOR THE
SMALL CROCODILE. ENLARGE 200% IF YOU WANT
TO MAKE THE LARGER CROCODILE SHOWN IN THE
BACKGROUND ON PAGE 41.

Body

Sly Fox
ENLARGE 200%

Tail

Body

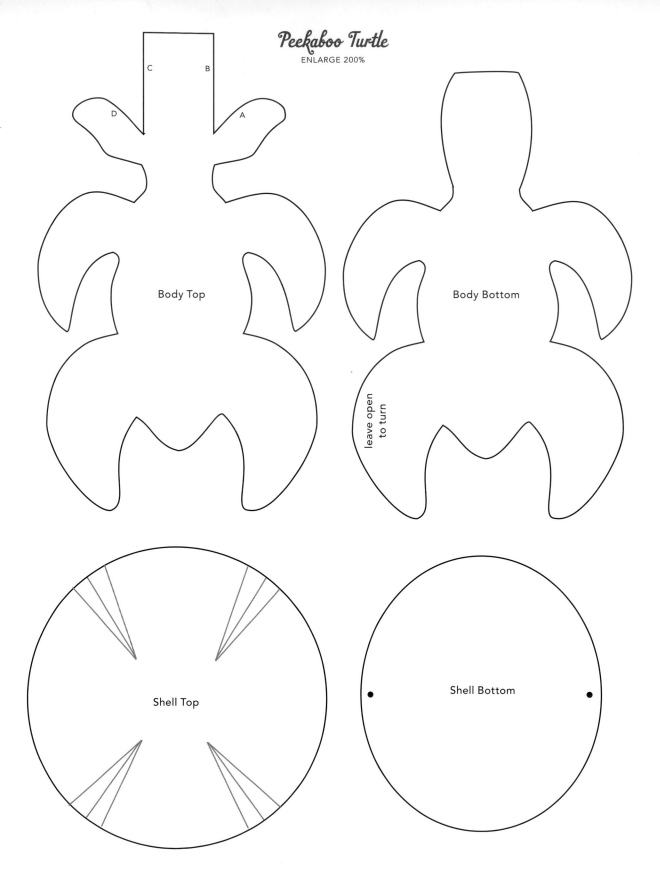

Peekaboo Turtle
ENLARGE 200%

C B

D A

Body Top

Body Bottom

leave open to turn

Shell Top

Shell Bottom

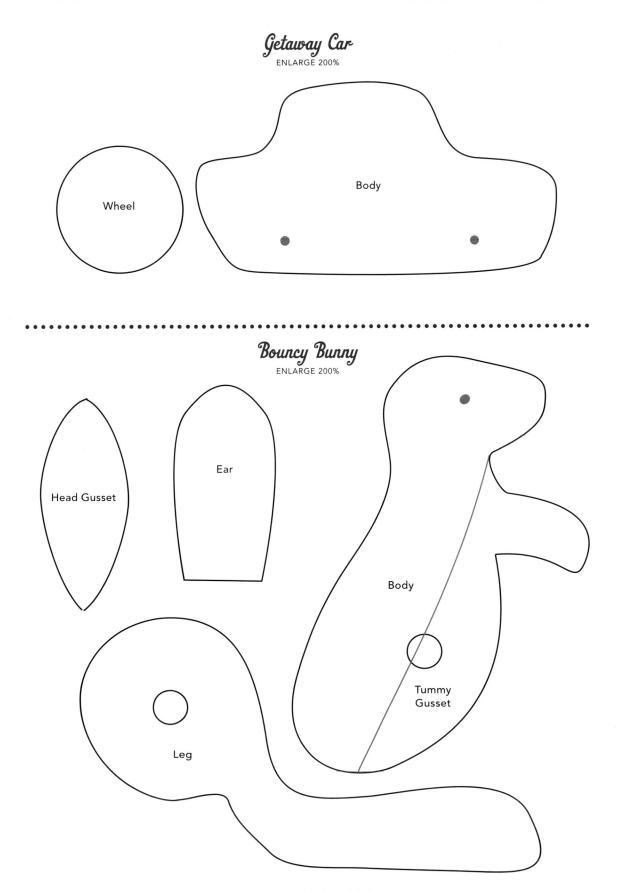

Getaway Car

ENLARGE 200%

Wheel

Body

Bouncy Bunny

ENLARGE 200%

Head Gusset

Ear

Body

Tummy Gusset

Leg

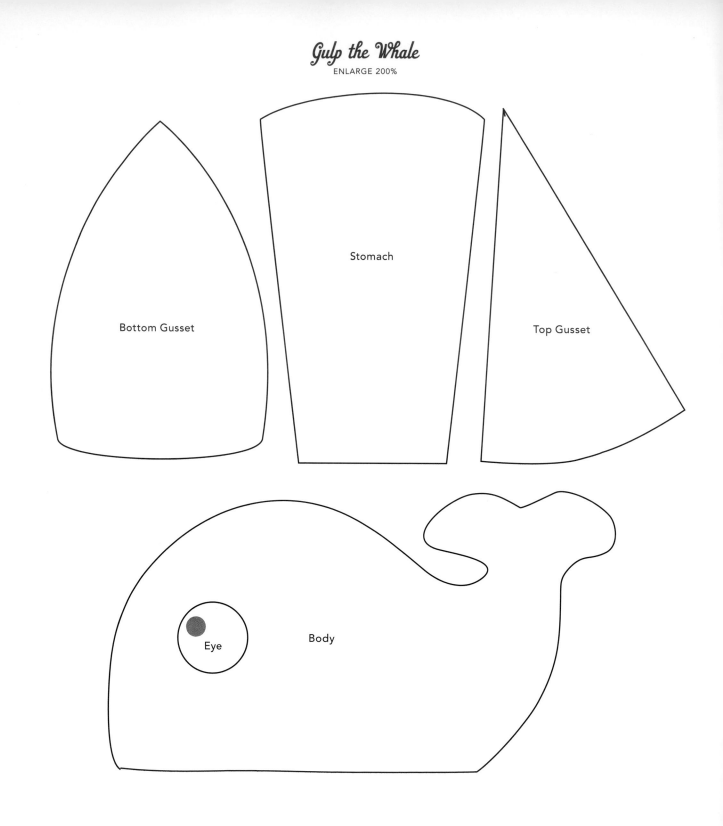

Bottom Gusset

Stomach

Top Gusset

Eye

Body

Winged Horse
ENLARGE 200%

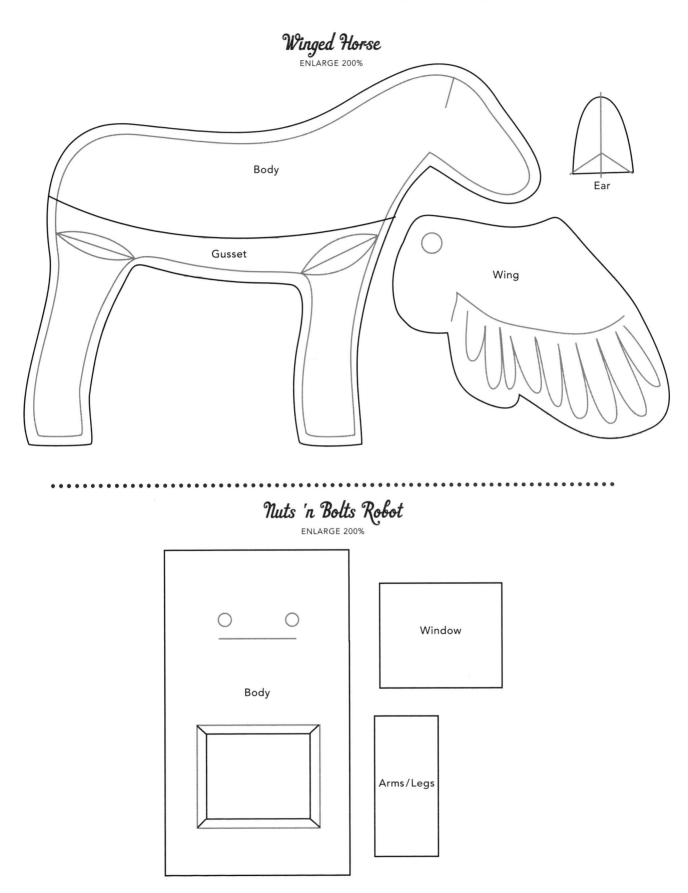

Body

Gusset

Ear

Wing

Nuts 'n Bolts Robot
ENLARGE 200%

Body

Window

Arms/Legs

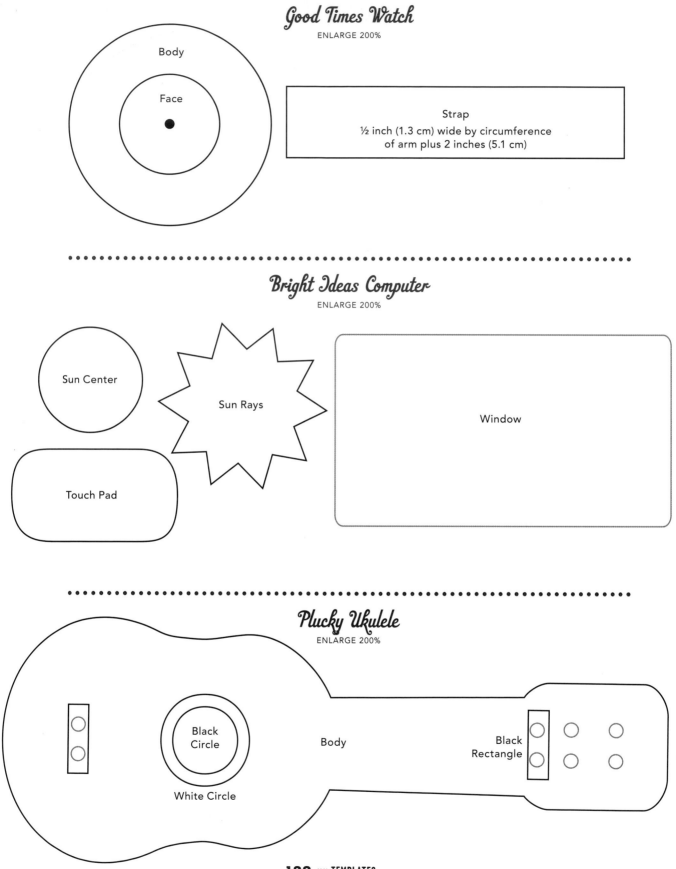

Good Times Watch

ENLARGE 200%

Body

Face

Strap
½ inch (1.3 cm) wide by circumference
of arm plus 2 inches (5.1 cm)

Bright Ideas Computer

ENLARGE 200%

Sun Center

Sun Rays

Window

Touch Pad

Plucky Ukulele

ENLARGE 200%

Black
Circle

Body

Black
Rectangle

White Circle

Grabby Crab

ENLARGE 200%

Claws

Claw
Gusset

Body

Back Legs

Front Legs

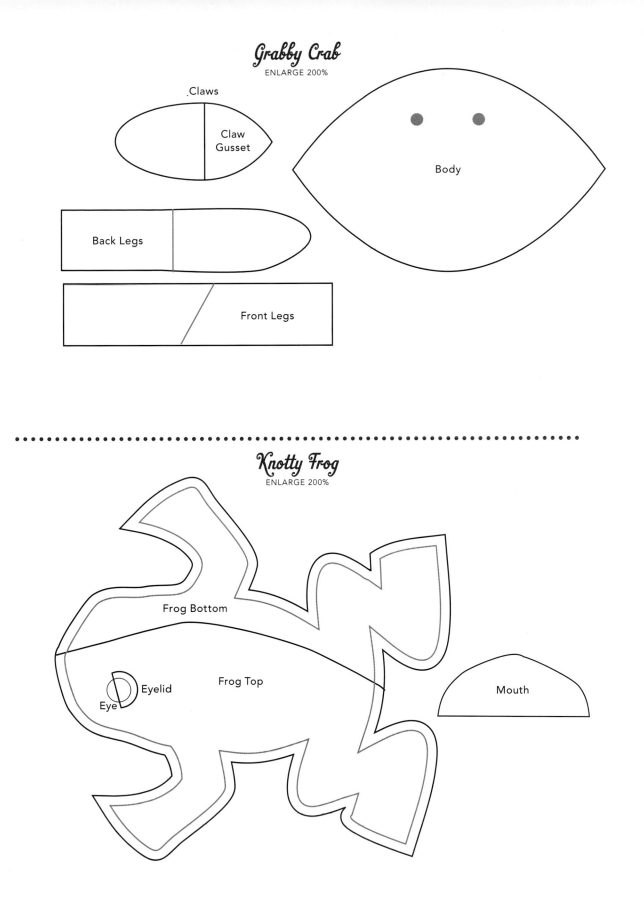

Knotty Frog

ENLARGE 200%

Frog Bottom

Eyelid

Eye

Frog Top

Mouth

Perching Bird

ENLARGE 200%

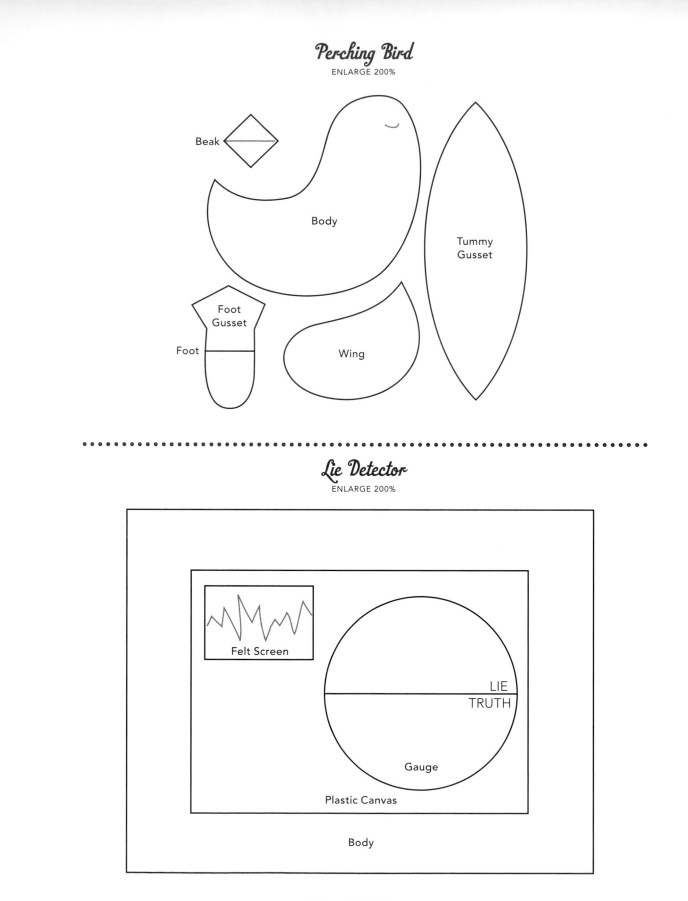

Beak

Body

Tummy
Gusset

Foot
Gusset

Foot

Wing

Lie Detector

ENLARGE 200%

Felt Screen

LIE
TRUTH

Gauge

Plastic Canvas

Body

Cat-Fish Doll

ENLARGE 200%

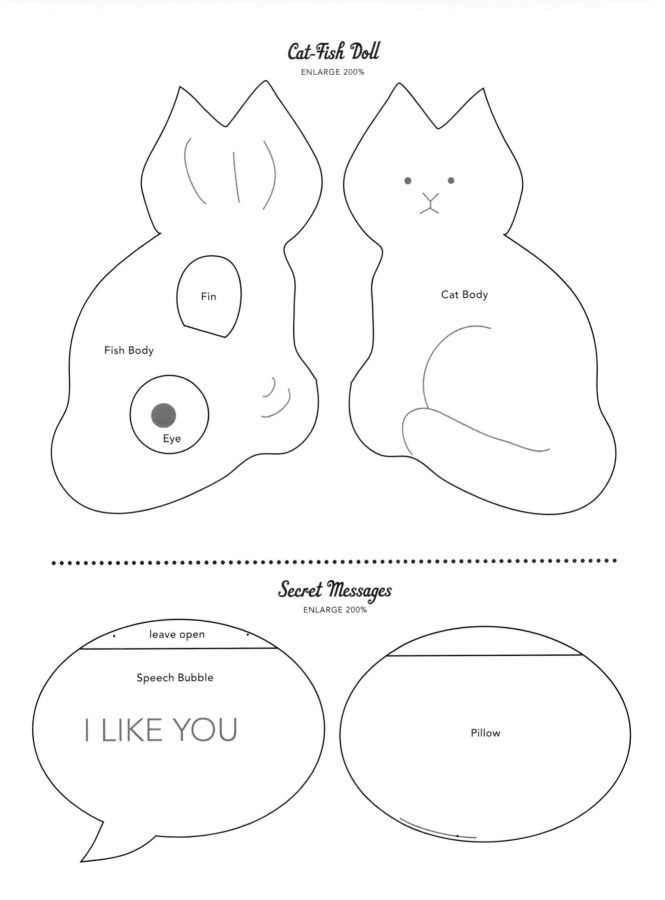

Fin

Fish Body

Eye

Cat Body

Secret Messages

ENLARGE 200%

leave open

Speech Bubble

I LIKE YOU

Pillow

The Caterpillar and the Butterfly
ENLARGE 200%

Body Top

Body Bottom

Wings

George and the Dragon
ENLARGE 200%

Arm / Leg

Visor

Face

Body

Waistline

Fold

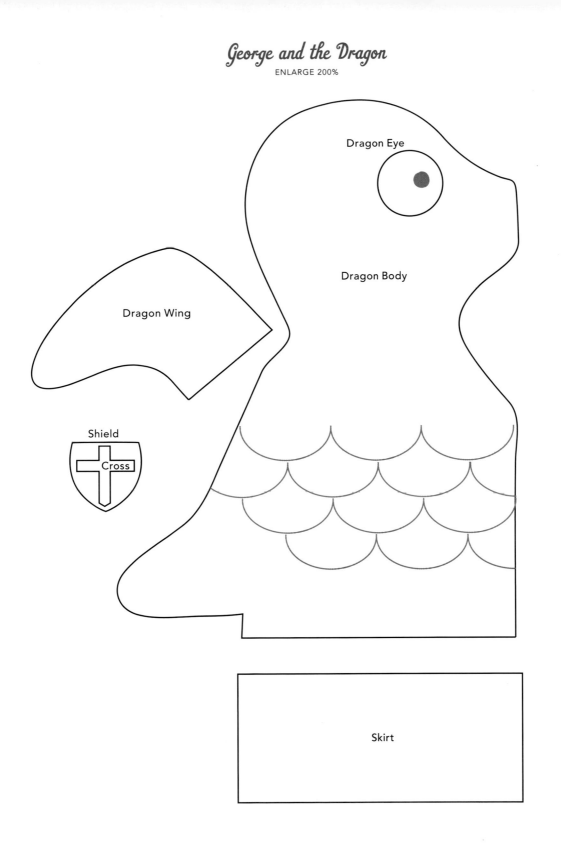

Dragon Eye

Dragon Body

Dragon Wing

Shield

Cross

Skirt

The Owl and the Pussycat
ENLARGE 200%

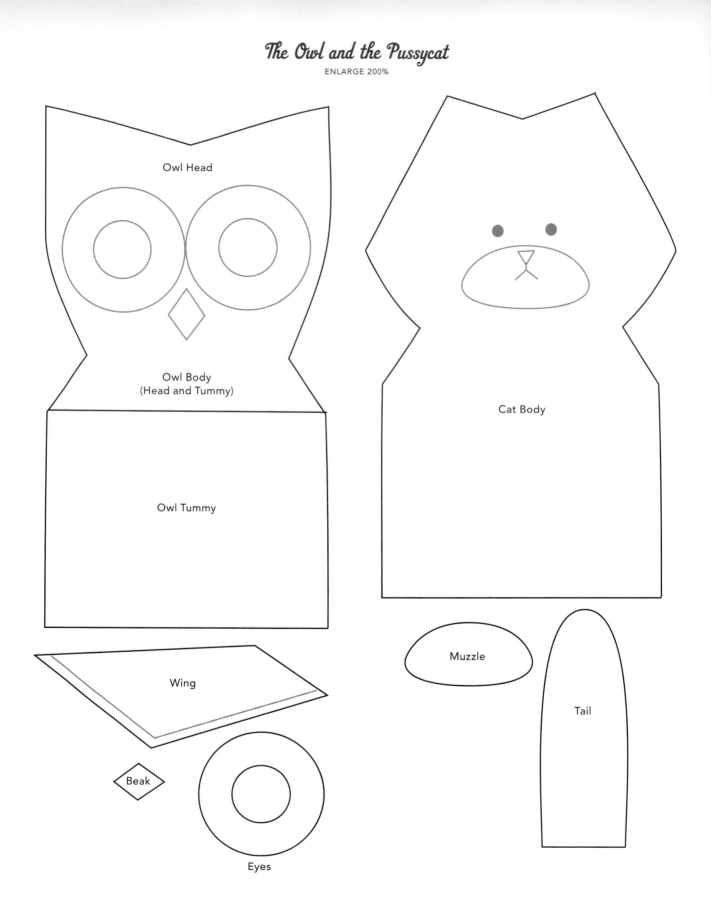

Owl Head

Owl Body
(Head and Tummy)

Owl Tummy

Cat Body

Wing

Muzzle

Tail

Beak

Eyes

Superhero Flip Doll

ENLARGE 200%

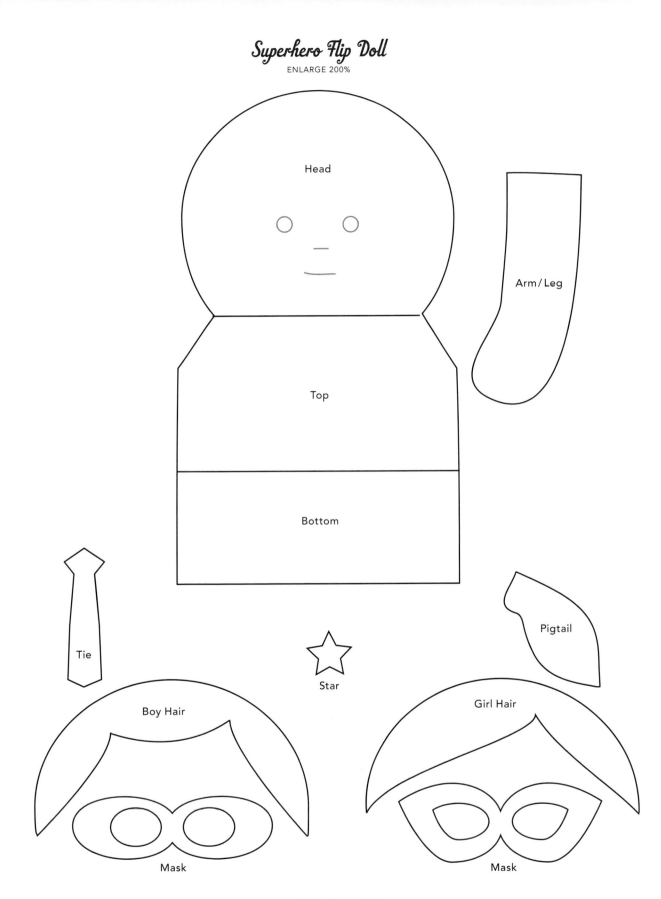

Head

Arm/Leg

Top

Bottom

Tie

Star

Pigtail

Boy Hair

Girl Hair

Mask

Mask

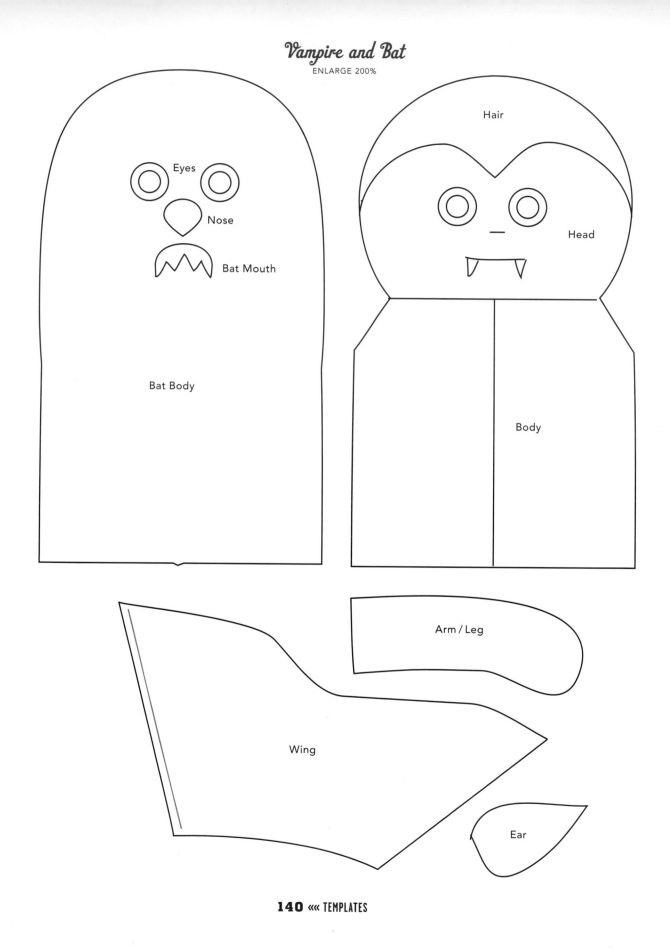

Vampire and Bat

ENLARGE 200%

Eyes

Nose

Bat Mouth

Bat Body

Hair

Head

Body

Arm / Leg

Wing

Ear

Circus Flip Doll

ENLARGE 200%

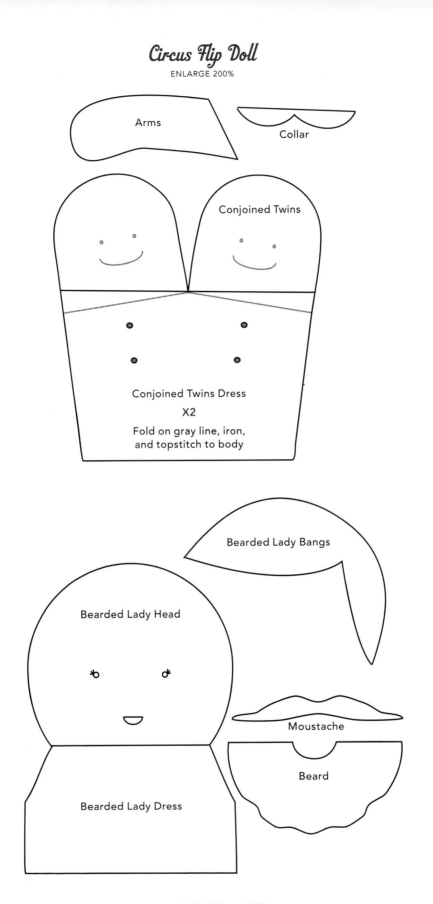

Arms

Collar

Conjoined Twins

Conjoined Twins Dress
X2
Fold on gray line, iron,
and topstitch to body

Bearded Lady Bangs

Bearded Lady Head

Moustache

Beard

Bearded Lady Dress

resources

SUPPLIES

I hoard fabric and notions that I find at yard sales and thrift stores. Often, you'll find a whole stash after someone has cleaned out her sewing box. Start your own stash! You never know when you'll need a bit of lace or rickrack. Vintage bits of fabric make great accents on the tummy of a bunny or the screen of a computer. Scan the aisles of your local fabric shop for interesting notions and complementary fabrics. Here are some other sources for supplies that I love.

ETSY

www.etsy.com/category/supplies
Check out Etsy's supplies category for wholesale prices on commercially made products, or hand-made supplies like carved wooden buttons and hand-dyed fabrics.

FABRIC.COM

www.fabric.com
When I need something very specific, like mustard yellow linen, I can usually find it here.

MISS LABEL

www.etsy.com/shop/misslabel
If you want to sell stuffed toys, or just add a personal touch, Miss Label makes small-batch custom labels.

SPOONFLOWER

www.spoonflower.com
To design your own fabric, or buy custom-printed fabric from other designers, Spoonflower is a must.

REFERENCES

A phone call to my mom is my most efficient resource! But if you don't have someone you can call after you break your third machine needle, here are some helpful books and websites.

HOW TO MAKE UPSIDE-DOWN DOLLS, by John Coyne and Jerry Miller. Indianapolis, IN: Bobbs-Merrill, 1977.

This classic book includes patterns of many of the traditional topsy-turvy dolls. It's out of print now, but can be found used online.

MARTHA STEWART'S ENCYCLOPEDIA OF SEWING AND FABRIC CRAFTS. New York: Potter Craft, 2010.

Martha's book includes helpful explanations on many basic techniques and is also loaded with projects of all sorts in her lovely style.

READER'S DIGEST COMPLETE GUIDE TO SEWING. Pleasantville, NY; The Reader's Digest Association, 1997.

A friend gave me this book in college, and I keep it close at hand. It explains the building blocks of most any sewing project with thorough details and excellent technical diagrams.

SEW, MAMA, SEW!

www.sewmamasew.com/tutorials.php

In addition to having a lovely curated fabric shop and fun blog, Sew, Mama, Sew! has many helpful sewing tutorials. I especially love the zipper guide and sewing machine tips. Be sure to check out all the great project tutorials.

WHIP UP

www.whipup.net

This is my favorite resource for keeping up with what's going on in the craft community. Kathreen Ricketson focuses on craft as it relates to art, activism, and well-being, in addition to linking to brilliant tutorials and projects all over the Web.

dedication

For my mother, who patiently taught me to sew, and my grandmothers, who taught me to make every stitch with love.

acknowledgments

Discovering craft blogs and Etsy and the greater handmade movement opened new design avenues for me while connecting me to a beautiful community. I've learned oodles about sewing and style and technique from other crafty women and men who make things for the joy of it in their spare time. This community has been my biggest source of encouragement, information, and inspiration, and I'm so grateful to be a part of it.

Special thanks to many dear friends who offered ideas and feedback, especially John, who is truly clever; Tara Sanders; Will Shull; Kristi Montague; Rachel Steele; Christa Bryant; Chara Watson, who always unplugs my creative blocks; and June and Louise, my product testers and playmates.

Big thanks to Whitney Mitchell for helping me out with the sewing; her craftsmanship is stellar.

I am super grateful for Lark Crafts, especially my editor Thom O'Hearn and his tremendous feedback, vision, and support. Thanks to Carrie Hoge for the beautiful photos and to Amy Sly, Kristi Pfeffer, and Chris Bryant for the smart design. Last but not least, thanks also to Valerie Shrader, Kathy Brock, and Julie Hale.

about the author

Laura Wilson is a designer, illustrator, and jill-of-all-trades living in the woods of Tennessee. Her creative work has been featured in many publications and websites, including *Craftzine*; *Sew, Mama, Sew!*; *Whip Up*; and *Kids' Crafternoon Sewing*. Find her online at WeWilsons.blogspot.com.

project index